strong songs of the dead

Fa　So　La　Mi

STRONG SONGS OF THE DEAD

The Pagan Rites of Sacred Harp

TH. METZGER

UNDERWORLD  AMUSEMENTS

Strong Songs of the Dead: The Pagan Rites of Sacred Harp
Copyright ©2024 Thom Metzger.
www.StrongSongsOfTheDead.com
www.ThomMetzger.com

Cover and interior designed and typeset by Kevin I. Slaughter. Copyediting assistance by Alex Kies.

Cover and interior adorned with details of Robert Fludd's illustration representing the nothingness that was prior to the universe, from his *Utriusque Cosmi* (1617).

Title, chapter names and any text from a shape-note tunebook set in IM Fell English Pro. The body of the text is set in Garmond Premier Pro.

First edition. Published July, 2024.

Hardback (ltd. ed.) isbn: 978-1-943687-34-3
Paperback isbn: 978-1-943687-33-6
eBook isbn: 978-1-943687-35-0

Underworld Amusements
Baltimore, MD
www.UnderworldAmusements.com

CONTENTS

Down in the Flood · 9
Glossolalia · 12
Front Bench · 17
Tribulation · 26
Loudermilk Road · 29
Strong Songs of the Dead · 37
Going Primitive · 41
The Shapes · 45
Sweet Affliction · 48
Gospel Howl · 53
Folkways · 57
Vain World Farewell · 60
Christian Death Cult · 65
Long Sought Home · 70
Off the Map · 74
Weeping Pilgrim · 80
Memorial Lesson #1 · 84
Nearer, My God, to Thee · 88
Easter, at Suicide Corners · 93
Battlegrounds of Memory · 101
Secession · 106

Genuine · 109
Gospel Gothic · 113
149 Watts · 116
A Thousand Coroners · 119
Ancient Days, Again · 125
Pure and Impure · 132
Intoxicants · 135
Disembodied Saints · 140
Raising Power · 144
A Stranger Here Below · 149
Utopian Trace · 154
The Whiskey Sing · 157
Ecstasy · 160
Jesus Is My Girlfriend · 163
First in Heaven · 167
Mr. Johnny · 171
Memorial Lesson #2 · 175
Ardent Spirits · 179
Hollis House of Horror · 182
Luddites · 185
Parting Hand · 189
And Must the Dead Arise? · 192
Bear Creek · 197
The Secret Schoolroom · 200
The Shenandoah Harmony · 205
Jesus, Then Moloch · 208
The Spirit Room · 212
The Traveler Comes Home · 215
Singing in the Heart of the Earth · 218
Memorial Lesson #3 · 221

Tune Index · 226

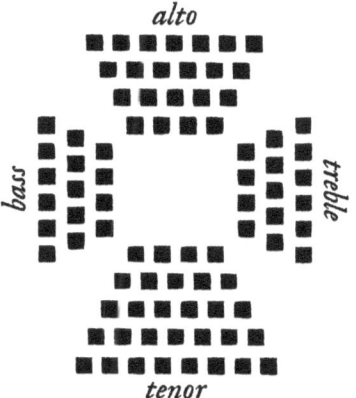

DOWN IN THE FLOOD

We sing for the dead and we sing with the dead. Untrained, unamplified, unrestrained, our voices are raucous and reverential at the same time. Our necromantic gospel songs are filled with equal parts delight and dread.

> Hark from the tombs a doleful sound
> Mine ears attend the cry.
> Ye living men come view the ground
> Where you must shortly lie.

The lyrics speak from a long-gone era. Likewise, the melodies and harmonies are throwbacks to an earlier time. But this is no bogus reenactment or fakey spook show. The dead don't rise in the flesh, but in sound and spirit. Their voices, their words, their *cry*, fill the air and reverberate in our bodies. Lungs, larynx, tongue, and skull.

Another leader gets up, takes his place in the middle of the hollow square, and calls out, "Let's sing on **page 397**." Quickly, everyone flips through their books, we get our pitches, and throng in together.

> There is a fountain filled with blood
> Drawn from Immanuel's veins
> And sinners plunged beneath that flood
> Lose all their guilty stains

What troubles me aren't the words. I've been singing about ancient blood and veins, sin and stains, since I was a little kid. What scares me sometimes is the feel of being sucked in, as if the music is a relentless riptide. At big sings, it goes on all day, and when the power comes down, it seems that I have no place to breathe. At its best, it feels like a wild flood, with waves breaking, re-forming, breaking again. And it scares me that I might disappear into it, a little fleck pulled under the surface, never to come up again.

I hear the summons—my name and home state—and getting up to lead, I call out, "Page 108. The Traveler." Fearful and elated, I face the iron-hard men on the front tenor bench. The church is arranged in a hollow square, everybody facing in, so that sitting to the tenors' left is the bass section, old men and young, mostly Alabamans, a few from Georgia and Mississippi. The altos, making up the third side of the square, buzz like the drones on a bagpipe. And on the fourth side are the trebles, who wail a skyward rush of harmony.

It's the first time I've ever led in the Deep South. I'm a Yankee, born and bred in New York State, and I make no apologies for that. Yet when the rough-hewn sound starts up again, there is no North or South, no old friend or older foe.

"Storm is gathering in the west, and you are so far from home." I'm singing as loud as I possibly can (and that's pretty damn loud) and I still can barely hear myself. "Rising tempest sweeps the sky. Rains descend, the winds are high." I'm the Traveler in the heart of the storm. "Waters swell and death and fear, sets thy path no refuge near."

We reach the end, and relieved to have gotten through this initiation, I return to my place. The next leader takes her place in the middle, facing the front bench tenors. She calls out the song she wants and with no count off, just the slight downward stroke of her hand, she plunges us into her tune.

To outsiders, Sacred Harp singing appears to be a crazy musical babble, the way it was in the old scripture days when true believers were known to speak in a hundred different tongues. Each song starts with meaningless syllables (*fa, so, la, mi*) which tangle together, weave and overlap. Then comes a pause lasting a heartbeat or two, and the words pour out.

Though many singers are introverts, there is a necessary *we-ness*, a crucial sense of *us* to Sacred Harp. It can't ever be a solo form. To make vocal harmony, we must have others, the physical presence of a group. We (and I, despite all my resistance, am part of this Great We) sit close: men shoulder to shoulder and women hip to hip. We, and only we as a group, can make these churning chords and whirlpool fugues.

Another leader, another song. "Page 70. Save, Mighty Lord." Within a few seconds, all the voices unite in a rising gospel storm. I'm lost again in the rush and roar, a retro-neo-pagan shouting once more to bring the ancestors back into our presence.

GLOSSOLALIA

When I was a kid, I heard people speaking in tongues in church. It was supposedly the overflow of the Holy Spirit's power that made worshippers gibber and twitch, babble and shake like holy drunkards. It was scary and it was fascinating, watching people lose control. Sometimes they let loose with faked-up Bible names: "Bahash shabala." Sometimes it was even more absurd: "Hundala shundala." Worst was "Shicketta, Shicketta," which sounded to me like angry insect noises.

Our preacher said it was a way to reach unbelievers, miraculously speaking their language. But I never once heard any real words in any real languages, just repetitive jabbering. Others said it was the tongues of angels given to mortals, literally the words of praise sung in heaven around the Great White Throne. Even as a kid, I thought this implausible. Why would angels make the sound of giant swarming cockroaches?

The only explanation that makes much sense to me now is that the Gift of Tongues was an out-flooding of subrational power. You cry out for the spirit to come with quickening (that is: life-giving) power and your mind will overflow with wild music and magic words.

Decades later, I heard a twisted echo of those glossolalic tongues. The voices rose from the grooves in an old vinyl disc, a recording made in Alabama in 1942. I'd stumbled onto this record at the library, one of a long series capturing nearly lost American folk music. Bringing this treasure home, I placed the needle with great care onto the first cut and out came a strange throw-back sound.

I knew a few of the songs from church. But I was mystified. What was this babble?

Then the singers paused, and started in again, with recognizable lyrics, and the song came into focus, taking form like a human figure coming out of a fog. I listened to the next tune, equally as mysterious, and I was hooked.

That was my first exposure to Sacred Harp singing. One taste, like my first fiery taste of Alabama moonshine, and I had to have more. Soon enough I'd sought out others like me who had a thirst for the lost and found gospel sound.

Pentecost—fifty days after Easter—marks the beginning of the Christian church. As described in the Book of Acts, believers from a dozen countries had gathered and were filled that day with the Holy Spirit. A great noise from the sky filled the whole house and tongues of fire descended. With this came a wild uproar of voices, a dozen different languages babbling together.

Some people watching asked "What does it mean?"
Others said, "These men are drunk!"
I've never seen literal tongues of fire when Sacred

Harp singers gather (and the liquor stays mostly out of sight), but the crazy confusion of voices gets reenacted on a regular basis.

Every time the square erupts in song, it's a mini-Pentecost. Even for Buddhists, lapsed Catholics, Quakers, Jews, and hard-shell atheists, doing the old Primitive Baptist songs means bringing down the holy wind and fire. Neo-pagans are also often represented at sings. I've seen T-shirts at sings that declare "Gimme That Old Time Religion." Below the slogan: a picture of Stonehenge with naked primeval worshippers dancing wildly under a full moon.

Many people, on first hearing it, say shape note music sounds ancient and primitive, something resurrected from the tombs of the ancestors. This is due partly to the style of the singing: unbridled and buzzing with discords. It's also the result of the open harmonies; that is, the chords missing their defining inner pitches. More than one person has said it sounds like a huge human bagpipe: basses groaning, altos droning, tenors and trebles keening the melody in a folk mode somewhere between minor and major.

On the most basic level, *The Sacred Harp* is just a book. But that's like saying that Moby Dick was just a whale, or the payload dropped on Hiroshima was just a bomb. It contains over five hundred hymns, first published in 1844 and never out of print since. However, when people say "Sacred Harp," they usually mean the entire musical phenomenon, the social organism with ten thousand voices. It has a continuous life, an unbroken chain of singers carrying the tradition all the way from its birth in colonial New England.

The reason it's called shape note is obvious when you take a look at the actual music on the pages. The note heads aren't ovals as in standard musical notation, but have four shapes: a triangle, a circle, square, and a diamond. These have names—*fa, so, la, mi*—and these names get sung before the words.

Originally, the shapes were there to help learn the music. But even if a song has been done a thousand times, singers still go through the shapes. It's said by some that this helps tune the group, bringing it into a greater harmony. There may be some truth to this. But singing the shapes has far more to do with primal outpouring than with good order and proper sound. In a six-hour sing, I'll spend over two hours wailing pure gibberish. That does something deep and permanent to the human brain, opening up the inner gates.

With all those voices driving the songs as hard as they can, usually a lone voice gets buried in the four-wall mass of sound. That's a part of the allure. Lost in the din, the ego falls away. The line between my body and everyone else shimmers and blurs to oblivion. At its best, I have the sensation that my voice is coming out of other people's mouths, and their voices are issuing from mine. This isn't just metaphor nor sound-drunk delusion. The resonant chambers in the head, throat, and lungs truly are affected by sounds surrounding and supporting them. The bones of my skull vibrate like a set of interlocking gongs.

When the chairman stands up to say we'll take a ten-minute break, it's like I'm waking from a trance. Time itself vanishes in the lost and found sound.

The chairman is a big guy, in every way. Extra loud, tall, broad in the chest and belly. His brush cut is more gray than blond. He adds, "We got a fine lot of singers today, and some people from far away, so make sure you move off the front benches to give everybody a chance to drink straight from the well."

FRONT BENCH

William Blake, in his *Marriage of Heaven and Hell*, got it right: "The road of excess leads to the palace of wisdom." Having made my first pilgrimage to Sand Mountain, I was a wiser man.

The churches where I sang were hardly palaces in the standard sense of the word. At one, straddling the Alabama-Georgia state line, I could see daylight through cracks in the cinderblock walls. Another, much smaller, church had six piles of rocks for a foundation. No electricity. No indoor plumbing. No screens on the windows. There was an outhouse for the ladies and a clump of bushes for the men.

Still, these places have a kind of majesty. No crowns nor thrones are present—only the brilliant glow of human voices.

Northern Alabama is where, more than any place in America, the Sacred Harp tradition survived the onslaught of progress and so-called musical improvement. While fashions came and went, Sacred Harp stayed the same, sung week after week and year after year in little

Primitive Baptists country churches.

Some people compare this area to the Holy Land, a place where saints, martyrs, apostles, and disciples once walked and prayed. For me though, it's more like ancient Greece than Palestine. And Sand Mountain, in the far northeastern corner of the state, is Olympus.

The gods there drive shiny Cadillacs and mud-spattered pickup trucks. They drink moonshine and iced tea doused with handfuls of white sugar. They fight with their fists (sometimes in church), gossip, hold grudges, get divorced a lot, and vote Republican. And they sing, as their parents and grandparents and great grandparents had sung.

They also ingest an amazing amount of heart-stopping food. Dinner on the Ground, as the feasts are called, is laid out like an offering to some corn pone God of Plenty. The endless tables, made of rough concrete, are like time-scoured ruins. Over them arches a crude shelter, the roof of an open-air temple.

At one singing, I paced off the serving tables. Over a hundred feet of food: the tables packed with scores of heaped dishes. Fried okra and fried pie, slaw, cardboard boxes lined with foil and overloaded with greasy fried chicken, pickled beets, BBQ by the bucket, thick slabs of cold bacon, butter beans, field peas, chicken dressing, red velvet cake, and a hundred other high-calorie delights.

On my first trip to Sand Mountain, I stayed with a guy named Kester Vines, who'd been singing from *The Sacred Harp* for most of his seventy-plus years. At his house I got another, more personal, taste of Alabaman excess. Kester is a big man, as fine a cook as he is a singer.

For our first breakfast he made up a mound of cathead biscuits and a half gallon of sawmill gravy.

That night, he seemed tickled that I had an interest in his corn liquor. So out it came, a Mason jar half full with clear homemade whiskey. Kester said it was about 150 proof. And the burn stayed much longer in my throat than ordinary whiskey. It was not quite as corrosive as paint thinner, with a hint of corn flavor in there with the alcohol flame.

That same night Kester got out his hot pepper sauce too, which he claimed had been aged twelve years. He'd found it way in the back of a pantry closet, the big jar all covered with dust, and thought to throw it out. But knowing he'd soon have Yankee guests, he'd tried it and decided, "It's just like moonshine. It gets better with age."

Much of the time, Kester's speech was difficult to understand. Partly that was because of how few teeth he had left in his head. He was as big around as a 55-gallon drum and wore overalls and no shirt. He sent me a letter after my first visit. It looked like the scrawl of an eight-year-old who'd already dropped out of school and started plowing his daddy's fields. Dwelling on this may seem like the sneering of a snotty northerner, confirming all the clichés about Alabama pig farmers. Nonetheless it's true, and none of it prevented Kester from becoming my friend and mentor. He was a genial and welcoming host. He put his guests up in his home on Sand Mountain and seemed to enjoy our visit. Yankees or not, we came to sing from *The Sacred Harp* and that was all that mattered to him.

His hearing and vision were not what they used to be. And his voice had suffered too over the years. Still, his presence on the front tenor bench at singings was vital.

I was well aware of the importance of this place in the hollow square, knowing that it would be presumptuous for me to sit up there at first. Some of the men had been singing on the front bench before I was born. As an outsider, taking this place of honor would be an insult to them, and to the tradition itself. Though the gender lines have blurred somewhat since the olden days, I still felt that the front bench was the place of men, men who've proved themselves worthy.

One of the first sings Kester took me to was a short Friday night gathering in Huntsville. Out of deference, I sat back a few rows.

After I'd led **"Gospel Trumpet,"** Kester made room for me on the front bench. I asked "Are you sure?" and he said he sure enough was. So, I sat up there and led with other men. Later on, I asked if I'd embarrassed myself by doing it wrong. Kester said simply, "You done good."

Later, I asked Kester again about sitting up there. He said "You're a front bench tenor" and that was that. I'd been given the patriarchal blessing.

Some might say he was merely being kind and welcoming, extending a friendly hand to a Yankee stranger. But it felt that a bit more was happening than simple southern graciousness. The fact that I'd not shrunk from his moonshine and catheads, cholesterol-laden gravy and cracklin corn bread might have helped too.

At the State Line singing, a much bigger event, Kester told me I should sit up front before the singing started. This was awkward. I knew that other men of stature would be there and that they might think me an interloper or a rude northern fool, for sitting up there. I asked around: "Kester said I should sit up front. Is that okay?"

Another guy, with far more experience, said "Do what Kester tells you."

So, I did and the men there were friendly and welcoming. But at the first break I got off the front bench and made room for others. Kester asked me later "Why'd you move back?" as though I'd turned down a gift. I told him I thought I should make room for some of the big boys.

And he said "You're just as much a big boy as them." This was not true of course, but I was glad to hear it all the same.

At the next sing we attended, the stakes were higher and the sound a lot bigger. Inside Antioch Church, in Ider, Alabama, it was hot and damp as a preacher's armpit. Though it was nearly ninety and we were packed shoulder to shoulder, the doors and windows stayed shut.

What am I doing here, I asked myself. And why have these people accepted me, at least for a few days, with graciousness and generosity? Why am I sitting beside a well-padded Alabama truck driver, wailing my heart out about Jesus and His saving blood? From his cousin or uncle, I catch the heady fumes of homemade corn whiskey. From his aunt Lucinda comes an ear-reaming backcountry wail. **"Would He devote His sacred head for such a worm as I?"** From my body comes a similar gospel caterwauling.

The front bench at Antioch was a solid line of powerful men, five cousins who'd sung together for decades. So I sat in the third row. But even at Antioch the singers gave me a welcoming invitation to move up. After

I'd done a tolerable job leading **"Eternal Day,"** the vice chairman told me to take a seat in the second row. "Sit up closer to the fire," he said.

When the session was over, I asked Kester about the front bench. He said to sit up there "You got to sing hard" (pronounced *hoard*) "and you sing hard." Not *good*, or *right*, but *hoard*. The way he said the word carried a lot of meaning: hard as in strong, unstinting, not holding anything back. I think that after leading in the middle of the square, he saw not just that I could lead well enough, but that I would throw myself into it *hoard*.

Though there are certainly egos rampant at times, Sacred Harp is not about stars or individual talents. Though there are men and women who have the status of elders, without the others, the sound cannot reach critical mass. There are of course levels of inclusion. The folks out on the periphery are not as involved as those sitting closer to the fire. This is not so much about talent—or even experience—as it is about the willingness to let go and be swept into the ringing din.

Maybe it was the simple cumulative effect: three days in a row of eating pig and yelling about God, three days of tear-soaked exuberance, rapt focus, and skull-rattling volume. Maybe it was the fact that the Antioch singing is also a church service, with more formality, a kind of rigid, fierce Sunday devotion. Maybe my heightened state was shaped by my expectations. For me, traveling to Sand Mountain had the feel of a pilgrimage. I'd come to a place that might not be holy, but it certainly had the power of wild spirits.

I'd read Dennis Covington's *Salvation on Sand*

Mountain four times in the previous three years. Covington's narrative of his pilgrimage into the world of Jesus-Only snake handlers, had grabbed me, *good and hoard*.

He's a southerner, with some plausible family connections to the world of crazed suicidal religion. But like me, he grew up in a middle class, educated, and literate world. Yet within a few months of his first contact, he became one of the snake handlers and he captured better than any writer I know the wild abandon, the gain and loss, of ecstatic religion.

Even if I never got to see crazed Alabaman men waving rattlers over their heads and lunatic Alabaman women drinking strychnine, I wanted to soak up some of the Sand Mountain maniac vibe. I made a point of visiting all the towns Covington describes in the book, and during dinner on the ground, I met Lonnie Louie, who had handlers in his family. He knew, he'd seen, what it means to stick your hand in a cage full of rattlers and offer them up in the power of Jesus.

"My brother-in-law," Lonnie Louie told me, "He don't care about God the Father, or the Holy Ghost. You understand? Him and those folks at the snake-box church don't have no Trinity. It's Jesus Only. He says that's what keeps him alive."

Some would say it was the Jesus there at Antioch, whipping up the storm. Certainly, the men with tears running down their faces, the men praying out loud with their hands raised over their heads, would say so.

At Antioch the sound had a rising fierceness, as though the spirit were sweeping closer and closer. I looked around at the faces: happiness and passion, like we were all being sucked up into the vortex and we ourselves were that vortex, as if those hundred voices somehow tangled themselves together, coiling into a human cyclone.

At one point near the peak, an old man with a white whirlpool of hair on his head leaned forward on my bench and began a rambling monolog. He was consumed with feeling, saying that he'd seen us all "on the next shore, the brighter shore of heaven." I imagine he'd say that Jesus was there, fanning the flames, or maybe Jesus himself was the flame.

He stood up and raised his hands to heaven, as though warming himself at some celestial hearth. Then somebody, bringing his testimony to a quick close, called another song and his revelation got swallowed up in the sound.

What struck me then was the fragile balance between order and chaos. The chairman, though not the oldest man there, served as patriarch, in his starched white collar, his suit and tie. Watching him pitch the tunes, lead the less confident leaders, I wondered if all that formality, the rigid structure, was supposed to keep the passion from breaking out into raw chaos.

At lunchtime, a pair of middle-aged women, aunt and niece, started screeching and brawling, right in the church fellowship hall. They were big women, big with anger. And this was no mere hair pulling match.

Their feud, I was told later, went back a long way. It took four men to pull them apart. When it was over, there was blood on the serving tables and a broken finger, and the chairman was utterly chagrined by this outbreak. But maybe their fury was unleashed that day, in that place, because the feelings had been brought so close to the surface by the singing.

I didn't get tangled up in the dinnertime battle. But I paid a price for my wisdom: a double ear infection that made me deaf for days afterward.

Though I can explain this ear infection in simple medical terms (germs, air pressure in the plane ride home), there might be something richer and stranger at work. I'd gone to the mountain on my pilgrimage and heard. My ears were pounded by the sledgehammer sound and there should be no surprise then that I'd come away with some damage. Like Moses, I'd gotten close to the fire, and perhaps I should take it as a sign of blessing that my body, my organs of perception, were blasted by the power.

A week later, I was still deaf in one ear. Antibiotics and codeine didn't seem to touch this affliction. Doped for the pain, for an infection I'm not convinced had a physical cause, I was still wandering groggily through my experiences on the mountain.

My doctor told me to use a heating pad on my ears to lessen the pain. But I was pretty sure that earthly heat wouldn't be the cure. More troubling, I wasn't certain I wanted to be cured.

TRIBULATION

I lean forward, edging closer to the heart of the sound. I take a few deep breaths and get ready for my favorite song in the book.

About one third of the tunes in *The Sacred Harp* are written in a minor key. What is typically described as sad has for me another richer quality, what the Rastafarians used to call *dread*. By that, they meant depth, seriousness, expressive power. Of all the tunes in the book redolent of dread, the one I carry closest to my heart is **"Tribulation."**

It's short: only fifteen bars and two verses. It's simple, with no alto line to fatten up the sound. The harmonies are skeletal, doomy, and dire. It's a slow $\frac{3}{2}$ dirge-surge: like a capstan chantey sung by sailors who are hauling up anchor for a long voyage to hell.

D minor is called the most tragic key, and while the song might be written there, typically it gets sung lower, making it more reachable for ordinary singers. (Most tunes in the book are not sung where they're written.) Still, D minor is a marker: this tune has weight, power, tragedy, dread.

The first word of the tune is "death" and the last one

is "pain." In between we get a short, somber celebration of divine darkness.

Some newcomers complain about how depressing the words can be, and how bleak the sound. But the melancholy lifeblood of Sacred Harp pulses in a thick black vein. There is ecstatic release in the downer-drenched heavy metal of Black Sabbath, in the grief-stricken adagios of Anton Bruckner, in New Orleans funeral marches, and in the whiskey-bold keening at Irish wakes. "Tribulation" nods toward all of these doom-heavy sounds.

Until the most recent edition, the tune was attributed to "F. F. Chopin." And the note at the bottom of the page further mixes up reality and religious legend:

"Chopin was born in 1810 and died in 1849. He was one of the great masters of music. His last words were said to his attending physician, 'Now my death struggle begins.' He remained conscious to the last, and added, 'God shows man rare favor when He reveals to him the moment of the approach of his death. This He shows to me. Do not disturb me.'"

The quote is totally bogus and the song in fact has nothing to do with the great Polish pianist. The early compilers of *The Sacred Harp* were hardly scholars, and likely got the tune confused with Chopin's funeral dirge, which I sang as a kid with these words: "Pray for the dead and the dead will pray for you."

You can't march to **"Tribulation."** It's in triple meter, though it's hardly a waltz. When I lead the song, I give a solid stomp with my right foot on the *one* of every measure. Thump—two—three. Whomp—two—three.

And I sing so hard I can feel it from the bottom of my

guts to the top of my skull.

> Death, 'tis a melancholy day,
> To those who have no God,
> When the poor soul is forced away,
> To seek her last abode.
> In vain to heaven she lifts her eyes,
> For guilt, a heavy chain,
> Still drags her downward from the skies,
> To darkness, fire and pain.

In case there's any doubt, Isaac Watts used feminine pronouns four times in his eight lines of poetry. The mortal soul, the human essence that lives beyond death, is a *she*. This is no thoughtless or dismissive use of the pronoun. The most important aspect of the human being—the spirit—is female. The element that will spend eternity with God—or in hell—is devoid of a Y chromosome. No beard and no beer. No man-cave and no moonshine. The soul is a *she*.

Sadly, this she-soul can be forced away from God, looking heavenward with tears in her spiritual eyes, because of some unnamed crime against the divine.

It strikes me as strange, wonderful, and significant that in this tune, there's no mention of the trinity: Jesus, the Father, or the Holy Ghost. Death is indeed a melancholy day for those who have no God, but perhaps Watts meant that any god is better than no god at all. Does that then leave room for the soul to embrace some other deities besides the Christian Big Three? It's a stretch, but maybe it even gives backchannel permission to follow an alternate pagan path to heaven.

LOUDERMILK ROAD

Sand Mountain is actually a plateau, about seventy miles long and twenty-five across. In the northeast corner of Alabama, it's only a couple hours from Atlanta. It still retains some of its legendary isolation but has been steadily encroached on by the tawdry trash of modern American culture. There are a couple of dragstrips, plenty of sagging house trailers, junkyards, tanning salons and tattoo parlors mixed in with the collapsing chicken coops and burnt-out barns. Some farmers have found it more profitable to raise cannabis, rather than the traditional corn and sorghum. We saw a lot of churches (some converted from abandoned gas stations, and some with flickering U-Haul signs by the roadside—"Get Good Religion!") and heard rumors about illegal cockfighting. Coming from western New York State, I was amused to see a place in Alabama offering Genuine Buffalo Wings.

Kester tried his best to ignore this slide into modern Crap Culture. On my return to Sand Mountain, he gave an informal tour of his area, proud of his cows, and pointing out the porch on the house where he courted his wife. "I'm telling you, son, in those days it was the most peaceful place in the world."

Then he took us to a cemetery where some of his ancestors are buried. "The state line runs right through. Over on that side is Georgia, and on this side is Alabama. Different time zone. You step over the line and you go back an hour." He seemed to like this, and wanted us to like it too.

Back in the car, he said, "You got to meet my Uncle Clegg. He used to be a mighty fine singer. But that was a long time ago." We go to another farm and Kester brings us into the kitchen, which is clearly the most important room in the house. "We got some visitors from up north. This here is Thom and his wife Eileen. And you remember Laura, don't you? Come for the singing." By the look of him, Uncle Clegg might remember ancient Egypt better than a guest from up north. He could be a three-thousand-year-old mummy, wrapped up in blankets, even though it's over ninety degrees. He barely moves. I shake his hand, careful not to break it off.

"Come for the singing," Kester says again, louder. "From up north." Uncle Clegg used to be a powerful front bench tenor and sang with a lot of Sacred Harp royalty. Densons, Wootens, McGraws and Creels—the families who'd maintained the tradition since the nineteenth century. But age and complications from diabetes have kept him away from the hollow square for a long time.

After a bit of small talk with his niece, encouraging her to come to the next singing, Kester says we should be going. We head out again in his Cadillac. Laura, our friend from Pennsylvania who'd made the connection for us to stay on Sand Mountain, gets in front with Kester. Eileen and I are in back.

Though there's no traffic visible in any direction, Kester comes to a full stop at a quiet crossroads. The rusted sign says "Loudermilk Road." Pines and farmland stretch off in every direction.

"Loudermilk," I say to Eileen, "that was the Louvin Brothers' real name."

Kester turns and looks back at me. "How'd you know about that?"

"I'm a big fan. I've got a stack of their records."

"That so?" he asks, clearly surprised.

"Yeah. Ira and Charlie Louvin. They're my favorite country singers." This is no lie. I own almost everything they recorded.

"Well," Kester says, "then you're okay by me. A Yankee who loves the Louvin Brothers. I went to school with them. They're the biggest thing that ever come out of here." This too is true. Ira and Charlie Louvin (née Loudermilk) were the greatest brother-harmony duet in country music: stronger than the Blue Sky Boys, sweeter and truer than the Monroes, ten years before the Everlys. Their album *Satan is Real* has one of the best covers of all time: the two brothers (in snazzy white linen suits, pink shirts and black ties) standing with their arms outstretched, wailing about damnation. Behind them are the fires of hell (actually tires doused with kerosene and set ablaze for the photo shoot) and a fifteen-foot, bright red, cross-eyed Satan.

"I've got a friend in Detroit," I say, "who's going to die with envy when I tell them about this. He was the one who introduced me to the Louvins."

Over the years, he had sent me hundreds of cassettes and CDs of recorded music: dupes of entire albums and transcriptions of 78 rpm singles he'd found in resale shops. The variety was as bewildering as the sheer amount of recorded sounds: Brazilian psychedelia, Baptist sermon-screamers (both black and white), trombone shout bands, dirty blues, dirtier funk, and bizarre one-offs such as a whole record of babies crying (with analytical comments), people possessed by demons, an endless audio report on the "Paul Is Dead" rumor, and *Ghetto Reality*, a record made here in Rochester by a group of tin-eared pubescent school kids.

The audio flotsam and offscourings kept coming, but what mattered most were the stacks of country music he copied and sent: the complete Hank Williams, David Allen Coe's obnoxious spew, the Carter Family, a dozen discs of Johnny Cash, and the Louvin Brothers complete.

Kester makes a detour to show me the place where the brothers grew up. "Charlie started a summer music stage right here. He wanted to make it big, so people would come from all around. It was supposed to be like another Nashville." The place looks desolate, empty, lost. No one's performed on the wooden stage in years. "Didn't work out. But they're still famous here. Charlie comes back ever' once in a while. Ira passed on a long time ago." The older brother—who vacillated between preaching the gospel and drunken brawls—had been shot repeatedly by his second of four wives. He survived those wounds, but got himself killed on the highway in 1963, traveling back home to Sand Mountain from a show in Missouri.

"If I could trade voices with anybody in the world," I say, "it would be Ira Louvin." I'm not sucking up to Kester. This is the unvarnished, unfiltered, unrehearsed truth. There's never been a better high lonesome tenor than Ira.

He is also a perfect example of the saved-and-doomed southern singer. He wrote and performed with complete sincerity such gospel tunes as "I Like the Christian Life" and "The Angels Rejoiced Last Night." Yet he drank hard and heavy, had fits of rage against his fans and his brother Charlie (famously heaving mandolins across stages when he couldn't get them to stay in tune), brawling and driving like a madman. Charlie was convinced that Ira was "under conviction." That is, knowing he was called to the path of righteousness but perpetually heading down the road to spiritual ruin.

Some sadness leaks into the moment: Kester and his guests thinking about Ira, long gone, and Charlie's failed stage there at the end of Loudermilk Road.

On the way back to Kester's place, he detours to show us a pretty little country church. "Plenty of good singing there in the old days." Then we pass through a small town. Waiting at the one stop light, Kester points over to the corner and says, with complete nonchalance, "My daddy shot a black man right there."

I have no idea how to respond to this. Do I ask him to repeat it because maybe I didn't hear right? Shot a black man? I want to know more, of course. But how do I get the story without Kester thinking I'm just a prying Yankee jackass?

He volunteered the information, I tell myself. Maybe he trusts me.

The corner is quiet, brilliantly lit by the afternoon sun. A little whirlpool of dust churns around and disappears. A Coca-Cola sign in a storefront window zaps and quivers.

"Right there?" I ask.

"Right there. Killed him dead." He's not bragging, reminiscing about the good old days, or messing with his Yankee guest.

The light changes and Kester eases down on the gas pedal. As we go by the spot, I crane my neck, looking for blood stains on the sidewalk. But the shooting must've been back in the '50s. A long time ago, I tell myself. A long, long time ago.

When we get back to his place, Kester announces to his wife that I'm a Louvin Brothers fan. This gets me points with her too. She digs out a stack of old scratched-up records and we take turns picking favorites to play. She leans toward the sweetest tunes. I'm more partial to the ones where Ira sings like a man who knows he's heading for a car crash, and then the fires of hell.

After the singing that night, at a church over near Scottsboro, Kester asks me if I want to drive home. "Eyes aren't so good anymore. 'Specially in the dark."

I say "sure," and he hands me the keys to his huge white Cadillac. I suppose this means I've passed some kind of test.

It's dark and I've never been on any of these roads before. I'm driving a car the size of a D-Day landing craft, with right-wing bumper stickers on the back. I keep asking myself, who am I? What am I turning into?

Kester says the singing was "real good" that night.

"You sing hard in a good old church and you can't beat the sound."

"You got that right," I say.

The next morning, I'm up early and it's just the two of us in the kitchen. Kester is frying his homemade whole hog sausage and putting cathead biscuits into the oven. "So," he says, looking me right in the eyes, "you a city boy or a country boy?" Not exactly an accusation, but more than idle talk over breakfast.

I'm not sure how to answer. He doesn't give me the third option: "suburban."

"Well Rochester, the whole county, has three quarters of a million people."

This doesn't wreck it between us. Birmingham is about the same size as my hometown. And it's only an hour and a half drive from Kester's farm on Sand Mountain.

"So, what do you do up there?"

"I'm a teacher."

"Little kids?"

"No—big kids." I figure using the word "professor" won't get me anything good. And there's definitely no point in saying I'm a writer.

"How long you been listening to the Louvin Brothers?"

"Years."

"What's your best song?" He means favorite. It's not a test; he genuinely wants to find out.

If I knew only a little about the Louvins, I'd talk about *Satan is Real*, by far their most famous album. But I own their more obscure recordings too, including airchecks from their short-lived radio show: Songs That Tell a Story. "I'd have to go with 'In the Pines.' I play that one a lot." Ira wrote most of the Louvins' repertoire. "In the Pines," however, got handed down from singer to singer on Sand Mountain before the brothers were born. It's the standout track on their first album, *Tragic Songs of Life*.

"That's a good one for sure. A real good one."

Unlike most of the Louvins' best material, "In the Pines" has no religious content. It's mostly shadow, cold wind, and the high lonesome wail. Until this little interchange I hadn't noticed how Kester, for all his love of Sacred Harp, hardly ever talked about religion. Singing, yes. Which churches have the best sound, yes. And of course food, though he's coy about the recipe for his famous barbecue.

The name of Jesus, at least when I'm around, is never spoken in Kester's house. The Bible too is unmentioned. Other than *The Sacred Harp* and a stack of farm machinery catalogs, there's no reading material at his place.

In short, Kester does his Jesus business strictly at church.

There's an uneasy balance between privacy and public declaration for Kester. I sense no embarrassment or doubt. He knows where he's heading (to walk the golden streets in heaven). Yet he acknowledges that in the old days he traveled too many lost highways buzzed on amphetamines.

Kester drove truck cross-country back in the handful-of-pep-pills days. "You had to eat bennies like M and M's if you wanted to make any money." He's not proud of his former life on the road. But he's also not apologetic. "I had a wife and kids to take care of. I did what I had to do."

Kester is back in church now, and he'll stay there until he dies.

STRONG SONGS OF THE DEAD

I've been collecting gravestone poetry for years, preserving it just for myself in a small spiral notebook. This is not a scholarly pursuit, but a secret repository of dire rhymes.

What has withstood two hundred brutal winters is quickly being destroyed by acid rain and weed whippers. The poems are usually at the bottom of the stones, and carved in smaller script, more shallow than the names and dates. After two hundred years, some stones have sunk into the earth, burying these American hieroglyphics.

On one of my graveyard jaunts out into the country, I had a revelation. The cemetery had a fine commanding position on the crest of a hill. Below us stretched Conesus—the westernmost of the eleven Finger Lakes. A pellucid calm poured across the valley, a cool amber ache from an earlier time.

Eileen and I sat a long time trying to decipher the inscription on an almost lost stone. "Died 1827." That much was clear. Using a stick, I dug back the earth. The stone lay flat, encroached on all sides by sod, an old wound healing from the edges. I ran my fingertips in the crumbling grooves, as though the words might communicate themselves directly to my nervous system. The first line was complete: "Death, like an overflowing stream."

Western New York State wasn't settled by whites until long after New England, so there's far less Puritan doom in the graveyard poetry here than on the far side of the Hudson River. Still, at times I discover a phrase that rings like an ancient iron bell:

> mortals be silent
> the burning flesh
> promises of blood
> cold icy arms
> sleep in dust
> join the long retreat
> one thing is needful

The image of death as a flood wouldn't let Eileen and me alone. We worked and worked that afternoon at figuring out the poem. A word here, then a recalibration: "It's not 'blow,' it's 'flow'r,' with an apostrophe." Deciphering the ends of lines helps, as most of the poetry rhymes. We got *stream* and *dream*, *flow'r* and *hour* and those helped us fill in the rest.

Back home, it hit Eileen that the inscription felt like song lyrics. Digging through her *Sacred Harp*, she searched for "an overflowing stream." It took a while, but she's careful and persistent. Yes, it was there: an epitaph and a song. Words sung on that hill two hundred years before, then carved in stone for us to find.

"There are two of them," she said, working her way along the thread of lyrical connections. She was right: the book contains a pair of nineteenth century hymns that employ these words. One song is called "Mortality." The other is "Exit." Nothing subtle about those titles.

> Death, like an overflowing stream,
> Sweeps us away; our life's a dream,
> An empty tale, a morning flow'r,
> Cut down and withered in an hour.

It wasn't until that moment that I understood. The words, written by Isaac Watts, were meant to be sung, and they have been for centuries. They also can be found on gravestones, thousands of them, in little rural cemeteries from the deep south to the far north.

Why leave these particular words? Of all the sayings one could use as a parting message, the dying person, or his loved ones, had chosen this verse.

The revelation hit me: they're not lessons to be learned, or messages from the other side, but spells to be sung. These are the Strong Songs of the Dead, preserved in stone.

The Sacred Harp itself is a kind of cemetery, a musical graveyard. Dead men's songs, five hundred and fifty-four relics, are stored up between the book's oxblood covers. The pages are both the bodies and the markers, arranged neatly, like stones in rank and file. There's order and there's disorder too. These stones lean and totter. Some were crammed into the spots where older songs of a different length once lay. Some are much visited, much renowned beyond the precincts of *The Sacred Harp*. Others languish, obscure and seldom visited.

It is, in short, a beautiful mess. Straightforward and obscure, banal and amazing, deeply personal and at the same time open to anyone, in the public domain. It's not just a collection of random songs, but an oblong box full of still-living memory. It's a reliquary, not only containing the words of the ancestors, but the melodies, harmonies, and rhythmic power of the old lost world.

No matter how many times I open the book, I continue to find songs that I'm sure I've never sung. Discovering these tunes is like wandering into a strange little corner of a familiar cemetery and finding an intriguing gravestone I've never seen before.

GOING PRIMITIVE

Sacred Harp singing survived passing fads and fashions because of its connection to one denomination, the Primitive Baptists (also known as Hard-Shell Baptists.) As George Pullen Jackson wrote in 1939, it remained unsullied because, being so isolated, it was "beyond the reach of the enemy" (meaning: modern America). A few years later, he claimed that "The Primitive Baptist freedom in singing is due to their refusal to allow instruments into their meeting houses and their renunciation of revivals and Sunday schools."

The Primitive Baptists pulled away and stayed separate from so-called regular Baptists in the early 1800s. Calvinist in theology and conservative in outlook, they maintained their fierce self-isolation. To this day there is a tension in these churches. To what degree do they open themselves to outsiders, especially to those who are drawn to the music but who care little for (or are even repulsed by) the dogma? How welcoming can they be to gay singers, Jews, and atheists, and people who don't wear clothes traditionally associated with their genetic nature?

When we planned our first trip to Alabama, our guide Laura told Eileen to make sure she packed a flower print dress that came well below the knees. My face was clean-shaven (a very rare state) when we left for Sand Mountain. I usually wore Hawaiian shirts to summer sings. For our trips down south, I had nothing so loud or informal.

Writing in 1978, Buell Cobb emphasized the "rapport" and "natural alliance" between Sacred Harp singing and Primitive Baptist churches, a few of which still use the book in their services. "But otherwise, apparently, *The Sacred Harp* is not anywhere involved in regular church worship." He also called the singing a "living vestige of the past." This may call to mind the shark, which hasn't evolved since dinosaur days, or something a bit less fearsome, for instance, two large ladies screaming, cursing, and rolling around on the floor in the fellowship hall (as I'd seen at Antioch.)

While *primitive* in the name is used in the sense of *original*, it conjured in my imagination something veering toward the ancient, the raw, the pagan.

I make no claim to down-home country authenticity. But then what does that mean when the percentage of the rural population of the U.S. continues to shrink and so-called country music is now produced by suburban pretty boys in expensive cowboy hats?

Trying to figure out where I stand continues to be quite a puzzler. In the negative column are these facts. I've lived my entire life in the Empire State, far above the Mason and Dixon line. I grew up in a suburban house with running water and a fully functional flush toilet. I went to a good college, didn't marry my cousin, and have retained almost all my teeth. The first time I voted in a presidential election, I pulled the lever for Gus Hall, the Communist Party candidate. I'm pretty sure that Darwin was right, and having a common ancestor with the great apes is just fine with me. Seeing a bumper sticker that read, "Jesus had two dads and it worked out okay," made me laugh. I don't own a pickup truck, never watch NASCAR on TV, and I've never gone hunting or trapping (though my extended family includes plenty of people who embrace all of these.)

The list on the plus side is complicated. I grew up in a church where they threw a lot of demons out of people who seemed to me fairly demon-free. I eat and enjoy collards, butter beans, corn bread, and barbecue pig meat, though I came late to the bountiful southern table. Now I grow my own turnip and mustard greens. I have knowingly eaten roadkill casserole and enjoyed it. I've been to tent revival meetings in the Bergen Swamp (where rattlesnakes still can be found.) My father, both my grandfathers, and all of my uncles and brothers-in-law did their time in the U.S. military. My mother married my father, and after he died, his cousin. Farther into the tangles of my family tree, two Metzger brothers married two Miller sisters; so, I'm related to my stepsister three ways. One of my best friends was dead in prison before we graduated high school. Another one came home from the county jail with teeth marks in his forehead. The meth lab of a third guy blew up a couple years ago.

I once attended a tractor pull near the town of Elba, New York State's self-proclaimed Onion Capital of the World. I must confess though that I took in a performance of Mozart's *Don Giovanni* a few days later, so perhaps that canceled out any points I got watching big imbecilic machines fight against each other, very loudly. On Saturday and Sunday this week I sang shape note music for a total of eleven hours. On Wednesday, Thursday and Friday I attended a pipe organ conference, along with guest musicians and master organ builders from Sweden, Japan, and Australia.

On our first foray south, I brought along a present for our hosts: a bottle of maple syrup made by a friend of mine. When I gave it to Kester, he unscrewed the top, stuck his finger in and tasted a big glistening dollop. "That's real good," he said, and seemed impressed that you could get something so sweet out of a tree.

But north or south, traveling out in the country I catch the same smells of gasoline and wet dirt from broken fields. Less than an hour—East, West, and South—from my house, I can find venison steaks and sausage, tattered song books, church pews shined by ten thousand buttocks, chainsaw carvings, and gigantic meals (call them potluck or dinner on the grounds) served up by fiercely bustling church ladies.

I have no desire to glorify or romanticize rural America. What's out there in the middle of nowhere? A lot of angry flag-waving, off-road motor vehicles, dog fighting, and hostility toward scientific learning. As compensation though you can enjoy some excellent dishes making use of wild game, charming churches, homemade applejack and corn liquor, much open space, tiny and poorly tended graveyards, lots of trees, and great music.

THE SHAPES

Some of the Sacred Harp melodies go back five centuries. The harmonies too evoke a lost world. Though some lyrics are banal Christian cliché, others take us into bizarre territory.

> And fiery serpents oft appear
> Through the enchanted ground.
> Dark nights and clouds and gloomy fear—
> And dragons often roar.

But it's in the *fa-so-la* clamor where the deepest power lies. Just the phrase *singing the shapes* feels irrational. How can a geometrical form have sound? One answer was passed along to me by an Alabaman who'd been singing shapes for half a century. "It's the music of the spheres." He was both a sawmill worker and a mystic, a hard-fisted and pine-gummed roughneck and a devotee of celestial harmony brought down to earth.

There's a baby prattle quality to the syllables. *Fa, so, la, mi.* Three vowel sounds: (ah oh ah ee) and four soft consonants. The whispered whoosh of *f*. The sibilant hiss of *s*. The sound of the *l* that's barely there. *M* is a hum in the upper palette.

Other shape note systems have seven symbols, and this makes sense: one for each pitch in the standard scale. But Sacred Harp singing is built on an earlier system. It's like a spiral staircase. Begin at *fa*, go up four steps and you're at *fa* again, four more and you're at the top, an octave directly above where you started. From bottom to top: *Fa so la fa so la mi fa*.

The shapes truly do work, even for those of us who started out on standard musical symbols, or round note music as we sometimes call it. Now that the system has reshaped my brain, I automatically translate any music I read into *fa so la* and *mi*. A Beethoven symphony or a kitsch anthem like "Stairway to Heaven" get recalibrated in my brain.

Understanding the theory is unimportant. The shapes permeate your brain long before they make sense. Again and again, we'll say to a new singer, "Don't worry about the shapes. They'll come. You get it by immersion, not thinking it through. For now, just sing *fla-fla-fla*. That's what everybody does." Only at special times do we go straight into the words. Singing the shapes is a bow to the tradition, to some vaguely remembered past. It's also sorcery hiding in the form of nonsense. *The Sacred Harp* is a hillbilly grimoire, filled with arcane spells masquerading as folksy hymns.

Catholics have their Latin prayers and Lutherans recite the Apostles' Creed. Buddhists chant in Pali and Sanskrit. Some unbelievers are instantaneously converted to Islam by hearing a short passage from the Quran intoned in Arabic. Deracinated Jews still sprinkle a little Hebrew on their holidays. Primitive Baptists have four simple sounds.

Pushing hard, making the bones of my skull resonate, I give myself to the shaped notes, and the notes give back. This might seem like mystical blather, but I'm convinced. Little black specks on a page, four shapes on a staff. They give and I give back, in a circuit of energy.

SWEET AFFLICTION

At the next big sing I attend on Sand Mountain, I get talking to a middle-aged guy named Melton during dinner on the grounds. His clothes are clean but there's no way to scrub the red dirt stains from his hands. He doesn't come very often, but his parents "loved *The Sacred Harp*," as he puts it, "almost as much as they loved the Bible." So, it feels good for him to show up once or twice a year. He doesn't sing much, just sits in the back of the tenor section and soaks up the sound.

There's about a hundred people milling around outside the church, eating little mountains of food off of sagging paper plates. Melton tells me not to sit on the ground. "Fire ants," he says.

I thank him for the advice, and say, "You know Kester, right?"

"Sure enough." He's not royalty, but everybody I meet holds him in high regard. His family has solid links all the way back to the beginning of Sacred Harp. Staying at his house gets me a few points. *If Kester likes this Yankee,* maybe they're thinking, *then he must be all right.*

He puts his plate down on the tailgate of somebody's pickup truck.

I say, "He told me his eyes are getting bad. He had me drive his Cadillac home the other night."

"Yeah. He's getting on in years."

I look around to see if anybody's listening and push forward. "Maybe I didn't hear right, but I think he told me about his daddy shooting somebody."

Talking about murder with an Alabaman I hardly know seems like a damn fool choice. But I figure I'm only here for the weekend and may never come to this church again.

Melton doesn't say anything for a while. He gives me a long, appraising look. *Great*, I'm thinking, *perfect. Now this guy hates me for a damn Yankee and is going to tell everybody he knows not to say a word to me.*

I try to cover my tracks. "He was showing me around and he just said it in passing. We went to see his Uncle Clegg. And we went through the town where it happened."

"Kester told you all about it?"

"Not all of it."

Melton gives me more of the examining eye. Then it seems like he makes a decision. "He really let you drive his Cadillac?"

"Yeah. It's a big car." *This is the best you can come up with?* I ask myself. *Big Car?*

"Then I guess you're all right." Melton takes a long pull on his sweet tea and says, "Things are different now. In the old days—this is what my mamma and daddy used to say—a black man would never stay the night on Sand

Mountain. They called it the sundown rule. Black folks would usually go all the way around, and that's a long way. Back when there was so much trouble in Birmingham—marches and strikes and whatnot—this is before my time—somebody asked Martin Luther King if he'd do one of his marches on Sand Mountain. And you know what he said?"

"No idea."

"'I don't believe the Lord would be with us.' That's what he said." Then Melton added, "They would've just lined 'em up and shot 'em all."

After dinner on the grounds, the singing starts again. Rested up, full of caffeine and sugar, people really are laying into it.

I notice that Donny, Kester's son, has brought a small glass vial and has handed it to the guy next to him. It's not moonshine, but peppermint oil. "One drop on the back of your tongue," he explains to me. "Opens you up." It's no secret, but not everybody is offered this folkloric aid to singing.

There's a treble, aiming right at me from the side of the square, who's so loud the side of my face feels hot, scorched by her voice. I'd had a similar experience at an earlier sing, and another guy who'd been cooked by the fiery voice said, just loud enough for me to hear, "Okay, you can turn me over now. I'm done on that side." Today, everybody's overheated and uncomfortable, but nobody complains. Armpits are getting damp and dark. Some of the ladies' hairdos are softening and falling apart. I'm starting to see some tears too.

The sound is just reaching the peak when the doors

at the back of the church opens wide. From where I sit, I can't get a good look down the main aisle. The singing keeps going, but people can sense something strange is about to happen.

The song is **"Sweet Affliction."** The leader signals that she wants to do the chorus again. When the song ends, I hear a fearless, almost-regal, voice yell out, "That's some real good singing. I could preach behind that!"

Now I get a good look at the intruder: a black man in a gleaming powder blue suit. His hair is titanic, swept upward and shiny, like he's Little Richard and this is 1956. "Oh yes, indeed. Sweet Jesus, I could preach behind that!"

The church goes dead silent. My first thought: *are you out of your mind?* Why would any black man walk into a room packed with yelling Alabamans? Maybe they're not going to lynch him, but I can't see how any good is going to come from this.

Nobody recognizes him. Nobody rises to shake his hand.

"You folks sure enough must love our blessed Jesus."

The tension stretches like the last steel cable holding up an overloaded bridge. But when I look over and see Kester, he seems calm, relaxed, okay with whatever's about to happen. Nobody—I'm reassured—is going to get strung up, doused with kerosene, and burnt alive.

The black guy doesn't have a message for us. No prophesy, no gospel exhortation. He likes the music. That's clear. He's in a good mood and has no fear. That's clear too.

Melton is right: things are different now in Sand Mountain.

At last, the chairman calls out "117!" and gives the pitches. The song starts up, and people are pushing even harder now, to make sure the black guy's voice is totally buried.

By the time we reach the end of "Babylon is Fallen," he's gone.

Getting in the car, I ask Kester if he'd ever seen the guy before.

"No sir. Not that I recall," he says.

All the way back to Kester's farm, I keep my *Sacred Harp* in my lap and closed up tight. Inside is the funeral home fan that I took. They're common at big sings. Mostly it's the old ladies with big hair who use fans, fluttering them to stir up a little fetid air. Usually, they're made of a square of pasteboard, printed on both sides, stapled to a thin handle of pine, like a big tongue depressor with wavy edges.

Mine comes courtesy of the Asa Goreman Funeral Home in Fort Payne, Alabama. Below the name of the proprietor are the words "We Service All Policies—Ambulance Ministry Available."

GOSPEL HOWL

My first taste of the sound—live and in person—had occurred in my own living room. Eileen had been given some photocopied pages and invited a few people from church to try them out. We didn't have books yet. We didn't even know *The Sacred Harp* was still in print. So, a dozen friends who had little idea what shaped note was had gathered, and we handed out the xeroxed music.

Looking back, I'm sure it sounded weak and tepid compared to the real thing. But we divided up the parts and started in. I don't think we sang the shapes. But once we got rolling, I heard the essence, the bellow and wail of resurrection. And when a chunk of plaster fell off the ceiling, I knew I'd found the sound. Admittedly, the plaster was in need of some minor repair. Still, this was obvious confirmation that I needed to plunge in deeper.

I do not have a pretty voice. Eileen used to say that I sound like a bassoon with a broken reed. This was no insult, as I like bassoons and I like instruments when they have an overblown, fractured, and frantic tone. With sinuses stuffed up for fifty years, there is a certain adenoidal buzz in my voice. Constant postnasal drip also contributes to my distinctive—if not attractive—sound. In other words, finding Sacred Harp finally gave me a place where my voice would be welcome.

Eileen said, when I first threw myself into the *fa-so-la* maelstrom: "It's a dream come true." She loved singing harmony and had done so since she was a little girl. I couldn't and didn't until I opened *The Sacred Harp* and joined my reedy, not-perfectly-in-tune voice to the four-part uproar.

There is some power in my singing, though I can't—like some young guys—strip paint off a wall at twenty meters. I had no vocal training until I was in my 40s. Though helpful, it did not sweeten or purify the sounds coming out of my body. I told my teacher that I wanted to sing "louder, faster, higher." She was not only a professional church cantor, but also played banjo in a Dixieland band and sang from *The Sacred Harp* too on occasion. We worked on my limited vocal instrument, and I learned some techniques for making more sound and causing less damage to my vocal cords.

At first, my vocabulary around singing was limited. I told my teacher that I wanted more control of my voice, and she said, "That's not the way I approach it. I want you to get out of the way and let your true voice come through." Besides the technical aspects of keeping a healthy voice as the years passed, this was the best advice she ever gave me. "Get out of the way." As though the voice had primacy over my thoughts, as though it had an independent life of its own. Her idea of the true voice was mysterious at first. It became less so as we worked together.

I brought a few recordings for her to listen to and explain what was going on. Chet Baker, the junkie jazz trumpet player, is best known now for his wispy, pallid, almost ghostly renderings of standards. On "Let's Get Lost" and "My Funny Valentine" he sounds like he's dead and come halfway back from heroin heaven. I also played some Ira Louvin, wanting to understand better his perfect high lonesome wail. He could hit the same high Cs as operatic tenors, but without the Italian showboating.

Mostly we worked on nineteenth century dead girl songs. My teacher had in her studio—besides two pianos—a Victorian reed organ, perfect for misty-eyed songs about young ladies gone early to the grave. These were all within my range and required no great talent or heroics.

Ireland has her whiskey tenors. Hollywood musicals of the '30s feature smiling man-boy tenors, pleasant and sexless. In opera, there are tenors called lyric, bel canto, spinto (light), and heroic (for behemoth Wagnerian roles). From light opera to the Beatles, from boy bands and Black Sabbath to the astounding Nusrat Fateh Ali Khan, the tenor is front and center. The word literally means *to carry* and in shape note singing, the tenors get to carry the melody, unlike most four-part choral music, which flips the melody up to the high female voices. This was also part of the gift: unlike in standard church hymnody, I can sing melody and be part of a rich vocal harmony.

On occasion people bring xeroxes of songs from other shape note books. These tend to have the more typical southern gospel sound: in a major key, sentimental, with little of the gravitas that first drew me to Sacred Harp.

Hearing her name called, a treble got up and passed out some loose music for a tune called "I'm Wandering To and Fro." She explained that there was a section "just for the ladies" (this is quite uncommon.) "So, if you don't sing in the right register, then stay out for that part." The song moved along and when we got to the special ladies' part, spontaneously three guys (including me) jumped up to the falsetto range and our voices rang out. The woman we surrounded on three sides looked stunned, saying without words, "What the hell was that and where the hell did it come from?"

There's something uncanny about the pure male upper range resonance, especially when three guys hit it together in tune. There were a few laughs, but the group mostly accepted the intrusion of this Other Voice that some tenors like me can conjure up. Trained musicians use the term "second mode phonation." A few guys, sometimes called roosters, sing alto at Sacred Harp events. They can reach the women's range without so-called falsetto. Some jokingly call this "mock castrato." Head-voice versus chest-voice: I didn't care about such distinctions. When the time is right, the gospel howl rings out, reaching for the gospel moon.

FOLKWAYS

Sitting at the left end of the tenor bench, I got an earful of some famous basses: old, weather-beaten, southern men who'd grown up with Sacred Harp. By then I was confident enough that I could sing my part and follow what they were doing. And it hit me that a lot of the time they weren't singing what was on the page.

They stayed in the chord structure mostly, and all their ornaments, slides, and syncopated entrances gave the music an added richness. But realizing that it wasn't how the parts were written, I also realized that these guys weren't really reading the music. And some of them, no matter what they might tell me, couldn't read music, at least not in the way I understand that process.

They'd learned the tunes by immersion, starting when they were little kids, and after decades, there wasn't any need for what was on the page. There were times when—song after song—the front bench singers wouldn't even open their books. It was so deep in their memory, in the fibers of their nerves, that the book wasn't needed. A number of new tunes, and some long-lost old ones, were added when the 1991 edition came out. And on those, the feel in the smaller southern sings was different. The work of northern tunesmiths, living or long dead, was not so familiar as the favorites that had been well established in the book, some of them all the way back to the first edition of 1844.

What I heard on the well-worn tunes wasn't improvising. I'd listened to thousands of hours of the great jazzmen doing spontaneous composition, taking standard tunes and making them brand new in the moment. The old singers were not doing such radical recomposing of the tunes. But literal and strict readings of Sacred Harp lack something that the looser, freer, folk renditions possess.

Singing with the book closed in my lap is a very different experience than deciphering the shapes and trying to fit in the words (which in some cases are a long way from the musical staves). Singing from the heart is a cliché. Maybe it's singing from the back brain, the spine, the deepest recesses of the cerebral cortex. With my eyes and my book closed, I can let go. And in that time-trance, I feel the paradox: only when we're in the present moment, loose and free, can the voices of the dead truly sing through us.

Sometimes in northern singings, it's a mess. People get lost, tangle up the words, miss repeats, drop out to listen or adjust a baby sleeping on a lap. If a singer goes too far from traditional practice, someone will announce, only half joking, "That is not the way of our people." Too much blathering from an extrovert leader and there's sure to be eye-rolling and someone who'll call out, "What's your number?" Or the pitcher will set the key again, good and loud.

There are times when we fall apart and have to start over again. "Follow the leader," somebody might call out. Or "Let's try that again," and reset the pitches to get everybody in the same key. Unless there are musical prigs present, it's no big deal.

However, there are singers both north and south who claim to own the music, by virtue of ancestry or grandiose academic credentials. They talk about "the way they do it in the South" as though there was only one South. Of course, there are hundreds of souths: from rural to suburban to urban, isolated and filled up with Yankee visitors, religious and overtly secular, black and white and Spanish-speaking, loudmouth right-wing and quietly liberal. The South is no more monolithic than the North. Hipster Brooklyn and hick Boonville (which gets more snow than any town in America east of the Rockies), the kitsch of Niagara Falls and the beauty of the Hudson highlands, the Statue of Liberty and the Cardiff Giant: it's all New York State. Dismissing me as a damn liberal Yankee makes no more sense than painting everybody below the Mason Dixon with the same broad brush.

At a small sing about a hundred miles from Sand Mountain, we were the only northerners present. Kester, on the front tenor bench, leaned toward Eileen as she took her place in the center of the square to lead. She called her page number and Kester said, just to her, "They do it in two here, *and fast*." This was both a kindness, to save her from embarrassment, and to let her know that there was no one right way, though the singers in that place had *their* way, and it was best to treat it with respect.

VAIN WORLD FAREWELL

We're off to Alabama again, but not the one in the Deep South. We're driving to Alabama, New York, a small town in the middle of rural, right-wing nowhere halfway between Buffalo and Rochester. Just a couple of miles up the road is the Iroquois wildlife refuge, where muskrat, foxes, otters, coyotes, and various rare snakes can be glimpsed. But I'm here for a different kind of wildlife.

Waiting in the empty gravel parking lot, I spy a cemetery down at the end of a one-lane dirt road. Nobody has shown up yet for the singing school we're going to lead at the church, so Eileen and I go to pay our respects to some of the ancestors.

Two hundred years after this poem was carved, we can still make out the words.

> Vain world farewell to you
>   Heaven is my native air
> I bid my friends a short adieu
>   Impatient to be there

Eileen wanders off to look at other stones. In perfect silence, I lean against an obelisk—cold stone at my back—and contemplate the octagonal steeple about a half mile away: three layers with a tin top, pointy like a witch's hat. Both the crypto-Egypto grave marker and the church spire point to heaven.

Soon, cars start appearing on the main road. From the hills and dells, the farms and creek-side hamlets of Genesee County, a crowd is coming for our singing school.

We've traveled a couple of hours into this backwater rural nowhere, to teach people how to make the gothic gospel sound that once rang in this landscape. Centuries ago, a thousand little churches were filled to overflowing with the raucous hymns. Long lost, then found, dead yet now coming back from the grave.

We'd expected a dozen or so people to show up and politely, timidly, join in. We ended up with the fellowship hall packed and a sound so strong it rattled the windows. Nearly a hundred country folks have come to learn the secrets of shape note singing. One large family of Old German Baptists streams in: the women in long modest dresses and head-coverings, the men with that macho rural swagger I'd seen among the Amish. A lady who'd celebrated her hundredth birthday just the week before has come, I thought maybe hoping to catch an echo of the past. As it turns out, she grew up in Brooklyn and had moved to the country to be near her daughter and grandkids.

On the far wall of the fellowship hall, facing me as I teach and lead, is a crude mock-up of Goliath. "That's exactly how tall he was," somebody explains. "Eight feet, three inches." He looks like Popeye's arch-enemy Bluto tricked out as a Philistine warrior: breast plate, helmet, bushy beard, and a giant sword.

With Goliath glaring at us the whole time, we go two hours. As the temporary singing school master, I do most of the talking, but Eileen gets up to lead too and points out elements I've neglected to mention. The class—and we call any gathering of shape note singers a class—isn't made up of overeducated folk music wannabes. These aren't people who've come for a little homogenized taste of the Good Old Way. They're backcountry Yorkers, shit kickers and church-going *pagans* (a word I use in its oldest sense: the rural rustic uncivilized folk.)

In the early nineteenth century, professional singing school masters would travel the back roads and pass along their musical science at week-long singing schools. They taught and made their money selling tune books. To bolster their sales, they often named songs after the towns where the schools were held. In *The Sacred Harp* are traces of those schools, tune names that read like the itinerary of singing masters journeying though New England—Windham, Worcester, Vermont, Natick—and west across New York State: Ballstown, Schenectady, Amsterdam, Poland, Russia, Liverpool, Pittsford, and Rochester, the city where I live and likely will die.

Origin stories are always a bit murky, but it's generally accepted that the first shape note system was created, and patented, far above the Mason Dixon line. Reaching churches where the singing was tepid at best and dreary at worst, from Maine to the Shenandoah Valley of

Virginia, singing school masters taught and led groups of amateur enthusiasts. Pushed out in the 1830s by the Better Music Movement (which emphasized restraint and sophisticated European theory), it made its way down the Appalachians to the Deep South, where it was enshrined in the first edition of *The Sacred Harp*. It was nourished, cherished, and protected in the backlands ever since. But the repressed always returns and the spark now glows again, brought home after two centuries in exile.

Singing masters still teach, though now for free, in shorter doses, and with a different intent. A memorable lesson for me was when a thirtyish devotee—who'd given up his Brooklynite hipsterism for shape note singing—led us through Deep Purple's "Smoke on the Water" using the shapes. We sat in a little church in western Pennsyltucky, a few dozen devotees and a smattering of uninitiated new folks and chanted the big daddy of all goon-rock riffs in unison. No words—just *fa, so, la, mi*.

This was to break the ice for people who'd grown up on early '70s proto-metal. We went right from Deep Purple's greatest hit to "Amsterdam" (named for the one in New York State, not the one in Holland). "Smoke on the Water" (1972), and then "fire ascending seeks the sun" (1742).

Preserved in *The Sacred Harp* since the first edition, "Amsterdam" is both Primitive Baptist hymn and hermetic spell. Though on first glance, it appears to be unremarkably Christian, in fact it exhorts the soul to fly skyward, drawn by pagan power.

> Rise, my soul, and stretch thy wings,
> Thy better portion trace,
> Rise from all terrestrial things,
> T'wards Heav'n thy native place:
> Rivers to the ocean run,
> Nor stay in all their course;
> Fire, ascending, seeks the sun;
> Both speed them to their source

The hermetic adepts put it more succinctly: As Above, So Below. Fire in the heavens and fire in the breast must someday be reunited. At death, the burning soul-essence is released, free to return whence it originated.

> So a soul that's born of God
> Pants to view His glorious face,
> Upwards tends to his abode,
> To rest in His embrace.

After our singing school, in keeping with Sacred Harp tradition, there's a way-too-big meal. Eileen is at a different table, talking with the couple who invited us there. I sit with an old guy who tells us that just the week before, at a church Sportsmen's Dinner, somebody had brought bear meat, which they roasted wrapped in bacon. I tell him I'm sorry that I missed that.

Mountains of high calorie animal protein, hours of high-volume unaccompanied singing, archaic lyrics with arcane power, a beautiful graveyard where I can wander afterward with my wife: if this vain world has something better to offer, I don't know what it is.

CHRISTIAN DEATH CULT

At the first local sing Eileen and I attended, the first person we met was a guy carrying a dish of candy. He introduced himself as "The Sugar Plum Fairy." I was just getting over pneumonia. (It had killed my grandfather and almost killed my father—I've had it three times since.) Under those conditions, it might seem a foolish choice to go in January into a barely heated room above a music store and throw myself into shape note singing. But I got through three hours, we bought two books and were back the next month, asking Laura—the Den Mother of the Rochester group—what was on the Sacred Harp top 40 so that we could be prepared for the upcoming big sing. Laura recognized that we were already fully in, and gave us tapes (labeled "a self-serving gift") to help us learn the tunes.

She was crucial to getting us on that first plane to Alabama. Having been to countless sings in the South, she made all the connections, set up who we'd stay with, and did all the driving, long before the GPS. The directions to Kester's farm—our first stop—were rather cryptic. "If you get to Flat Rock, then you gone too far. Go by the corner where the Big Biscuit used to be. Then you'll see a Meddigo truck in the weeds." (I assumed that Meddigo was a biblical name, but it turned out that our hostess was trying to say Meadowgold, the name of a dairy.)

Early on in our sojourn south, Laura (whose grandfather escaped from the Warsaw ghetto) tried to give us some reassurance regarding the hard-core Christian lyrics. "Don't be put off by all the Jesus and the blood. The lyrics can be pretty morbid and depressing. Just think of them as folk poetry."

Laura's attempt to soften the lyrics' power went unheeded, because unneeded. I loved the fact that I could sing at the top of my voice such totally un-PC phrases as "for they are not perverted," "I am so vile," and (the most shunned words in the book) "envious Jews." Offensive? Of course. But no matter how strange, archaic, or noxious, the lyrics have power. Sing as loudly as you can about "timorous worms" and "towering o'er the wrecks of time" and you're never the same again. These words don't just *mean*, they *do*. They change the world, or at least my inner world. I think of the lyrics as spells, in the oldest sense of that word: an act of speech or taletelling. (The word "Gospel" was originally "God's spell.")

Some songs reach an unfiltered and unapologetic perfection. "Granville" is a favorite at our local sing:

> Lord while we see whole nations die,
> Our flesh and sense repine and cry;
> Must death forever rage and reign?

"Liverpool" gets sung less often, but makes a similar exhortation:

> Remember you are hastening on
> To death's dark, gloomy shade;
> Your joys on earth will soon be gone
> Your flesh in dust be laid.

After a couple of songs such as these, it's obvious: Sacred Harp faces the Big Fact. We're all going to die; everything else is optional. You don't have to pay taxes. The government will just take the money out of your bank account. You don't have to obey the speed limits if you don't mind getting pulled over and fined. There's no law of the universe that requires you to reproduce or fight back to save your life. You don't even have to take another breath if you're okay with ending it right now. Death, on the other hand, is the real fact of life. Or, as a Buddhist friend of mine said, "Life offers us two things: itself and death."

All of this, some say, is morbidly unhealthy. I'd argue the opposite. Facing into the truth, making of it something worthwhile and at times beautiful, is the best we can do.

There are people who can't get past what are sometimes called the cannibalistic songs. One such guy came to us by a circuitous route, then vanished. I'd written a short piece about an upcoming sing for the local alt paper. Jim was working on a Nature Conservancy project in undeveloped woods in the Finger Lakes. A gust of wind came up, carrying a single page of newspaper out of nowhere, the page with my article. Jim peeled it off his leg, read it, looked at his watch, and made it back to Rochester in time to join in. He loved the sound and got along fine with the people. But after a few months, the doom and gore of the language was too much for him. "Eating flesh, drinking blood—I can't sing those words."

Others too have felt the dissonance of modern educated liberals bellowing about wretchedness and blood atonement. A guy from Virginia said to me he wondered what a person would think coming the first time. People sitting in tight concentric squares, roaring like a human calliope, waving their arms in time. "Do they think we're a Christian death cult?" That phrase stuck with me. The language is clearly Christian, the subject is often death, and there is a certain cultish flavor to the doings.

A favorite song that gets people up and really pushing is **"Cleansing Fountain."** The words are by William Cowper. In and out of asylums, a brilliant poet and a groveling self-hating sinner, Cowper captures in the lyrics (published in 1779) triumph, gross-out, and utter abjection. After a few verses extolling the salvific power of blood, blood, and more blood, comes this:

> And when this feeble, falt'ring tongue
> Lies silent in the grave,
> Then in a nobler sweeter song
> I'll sing His pow'r to save.

A dead poet six feet down in the dirt and rotting, yet still he's singing his mad glad radical hymns of salvation. Silence in the grave and sweet songs in heaven.

"Sacred Harp is not a Christian death cult." Eileen is clear about this. "There's genuine feeling in Watts' poetry when he's facing death." Grief yes, but also compassion and understandable fears. And none of the titillation, smirking, or dim-witted cruelty that suffuses so much of American pop culture.

"People are so alive when they're singing. There's the poignancy that life and death come together. The words don't pull any punches. They're up front about people's emotional response to the loss in death." Eileen doesn't hedge or hesitate on this subject. "It's a safe place to cry, and I learned that early on. We can mourn our losses in public with our friends around us."

LONG SOUGHT HOME

Eileen's sister was in hospice, dying, and we'd gotten the last call. "It'll probably be tonight." So, we drove an hour and half into the Finger Lakes countryside.

Jean had lived her last few months outside the village of Penn Yan. Across the road from her last home was farmland, much of it owned by the Amish who'd been moving into the area in the last few years. Sometimes when we'd visit Jean, we'd watch the black buggies heading out of the past and into town.

Jean—nineteen years older than Eileen—had been one of her primary caregivers. We were the last ones in the family to see her alive. By the time we'd arrived, she'd gone into the final opiate-haze, dreaming and fading, hallucinating and mumbling quietly.

"Who's that over in the corner?" she asked.

I didn't see anybody there, but I knew better than to disagree with someone who has one foot in this world and one foot in the next. The soon-to-be-dead see and know some things that the rest of us can only guess at.

As we sat with her that last night, watching the late

springtime dusk suffusing the corn fields, I heard a rolling motorized buzz. Through Jean's window, I saw a guy on a beautiful BMW motorcycle zoom into the parking lot. He was all in black leather: boots, pants, jacket, and gloves with crimson trim. The engine died and we waited.

A few minutes later, we heard murmuring in the hall and then the Man in Leather appeared in Jean's doorway. His voice was deep and raspy. "Forgive my appearance. It's my day off." He removed his helmet, pulled off his gloves, and asked if he could come in.

"I'm Father Frank X." (I later learned his full name was Francis Xavier.) "I've been to see Jean a few times." He was the perfect blend of solid parish priest, black leather Elvis, and a Teutonic Batman. I expected a rolling cloud of dry ice mist to follow him into the room. And maybe the rumble of tympani and the low moan of bassoons and cellos. He had slicked back hair and pointy batwing sideburns. He smelled of road dust, motorcycle exhaust, man-sweat, frankincense, and myrrh.

He waited a moment, a perfect dramatic pause, then said, "I'd like to perform the anointing of the sick." This used to have the much more powerful, and esoteric, name of "extreme unction." ("Extreme" as in "the end." "Unction" meaning: "anointing with oil.") I looked to Eileen and she said that would be fine.

Father Frank X. performed the ritual—simple and unadorned with any high church flummery. He took out a tiny container of olive oil, dabbed Jean's forehead and said some prayers. He asked Eileen and I if we wanted to join in on the Our Father, and I said the prayer as best I could.

Father Frank X. talked to Jean as though she were still conscious, telling her to "Just follow the Lord."

I saw something in Father Frank X. that I'd never seen in another clergyman. He was compassionate and cool, holy and hip. He was strange, other, beyond, and yet lacking in any trace of pomposity.

After a bit of silence, he put on his helmet and gloves and withdrew. Shortly, the BMW roared off into the shadows. The black leather and the extreme unction had worked together perfectly. German gear grease and anointing oil—the roar of the engine and the calm murmur of his prayers.

We sang for Jean—just of the two of us—as her time neared. She was unconscious now, hot to the touch, only hours from death. **"Long Sought Home"** is one of the few sweet-sounding tunes in *The Sacred Harp*. At a big sing, the last chorus is sung as quietly as possible, almost a whisper. Jean died not long after we left.

The next day Eileen and I co-chaired the annual big sing in Rochester. As I roasted pans of chicken drumsticks and made sure the church was all set up, Eileen was making arrangements with the funeral director, the florist, and the nun at the church Jean had attended since her baptism seventy-five years before.

At the sing, I called **"Long Sought Home"** and said, "I'd like us to sing this for Eileen's sister, who died yesterday. This was how we said goodbye."

Once the group started in, Eileen couldn't sing a note. Later, she told me, "Out of the corner of my eye I saw someone from the alto section come up behind me and put her hands on my shoulders, and even massaged them a little bit. It was as if she represented the whole group. I felt held and comforted by everyone in the room. The group was one in its embrace of me. They were holding me with their voices."

OFF THE MAP

For our trips to Alabama, I brought a "triple A" travel map and when I got home, marked all the roads we'd taken. I continued this each time we went south to sing, a squiggly black pen wandering across the landscape.

Ider, Hennegar, Fyffe, Section, Sylvania, Flat Rock: I wanted to see as much of Sand Mountain as I could. Barbecue joints, pawn shops, the charred skeletons of barns, and countless churches. The ones with no windows, I was told, were most likely to be places where they handled snakes. And beyond Sand Mountain: Tuscaloosa, Cullman, Tuskegee, Fort Payne.

Searching over a map, I saw a place called Dogtown, not far from where we were staying. The name was bizarre, cartoonish, and I wanted to tell my northern friends, "Yes, I've gone to Dogtown, Alabama." Mostly, the place lived up to my expectations. We drove past Mighty Warrior Ministries on Dogtown Road. We saw the volunteer fire department and a boarded-up honky-tonk called The Dogtown Fun Factory. Heading out of Dogtown, we got a cryptic message from the rear end of truck. The owner had placed two bold statements on his rig: "Jesus Answers Prayers" and "Caution: stay back 200 feet."

On another jaunt, we stopped in the town called Arab. Like so many towns in Alabama, there was a pawn shop in Arab. The sign in the window said, "Buy, Sell, Trade anything of value, but we don't rent pigs." I got up my nerve, went inside and said, "You can probably tell by my accent that I'm not from around here. I was wondering, do you pronounce the name of your town Ay-rabb?"

The lady behind the counter said, "How'd you know that?"

"Just a guess," I said. We have a Mt. Arab in New York State, in the Adirondack range, and people say the name just like in Alabama. Farther down the road, we passed The Arab Christian Center and The Lord's Supper Café.

Some of the songs in *The Sacred Harp* are named after places in the South. We traveled through Sardis (a few miles down the road from Selma), Jasper, Cleburne, Cusseta, and Montgomery. And we sang with people whose family names are memorialized in the book: Cobb, Jester, DeLong, Odem.

Bethel Church, in Heard County Alabama, is a gorgeous building used only once a year, for singings. There, I sat next to a guy who was over ninety and he made a point of telling me the church (floors, walls, ceiling) was built entirely out of old-growth pine. The grain is very fine, unlike any lumber you'll find today. Singing here was like singing inside a huge mandolin.

"Holly Springs" is another song in the book named after a place. It's another beautiful building, again all interior surfaces made of the fine-grained reddish pinewood. There, I sang with another very powerful front bench of tenors: Donny Vines, Terry Wooten, B.M. Smith, Jeff Sheppard. I tried to sit one row back, but Donny dragged me up to the front bench.

Hugh McGraw, the grand old man of Sacred Harp, kept calling Charlene Wallace, the leader of convention, "Mr. Chairlady." I shook hands with a 98-year-old who'd been singing from *The Sacred Harp* since he was a little boy. Another elder led us out to the real Holly Spring, where we knelt down and drank cold water from an old tin cup on a chain.

After the sing, exhausted and punchy, Eileen and I drove out into the countryside. We saw a sign that promised "The Greatest Gift of All: a drive-through nativity," but headed off in another direction.

Soon, we were on one-lane dirt roads. I wouldn't say we were totally lost, but we definitely had gone off the map and off the clock. At one point, we passed a hovel with a big Confederate flag and a sign on top proclaiming "Ku Klux Klan Home Office." We went past, then amazed that such a place could exist, I turned around and went by again. Eileen hunched down in the car seat, hissing "What are you doing?" I had to turn around again, to get back on the main road, so we passed this backwater Klan enclave three times. Three proud Aryan Knights lounged on the sagging porch, chewing and spitting. No shots were fired, though our rental car had out-of-state plates.

On Kester's fridge are a lot of photos. I'm surprised to see black faces there: three little kids who Kester's wife babysits from time to time. And a gray-haired guy with a fierce look in his eyes. I recognize him: he was from my part of New York State and had been traveling down south for years to sing. "You knew Allen Fannin?" I ask.

"Sure did. Fine fella. Real good singer. Stayed here a couple years back. We had a good ole time."

Allen was black. But the color of his skin didn't make a bit of difference to Kester.

"Did you know he got killed in an accident?"

"Heard something about it. Happens to the best of us. Real sad. A fine fella."

"Some of us sang at his funeral."

"That's real good. That's the way it ought to be."

Allen Fannin was one of the few black Sacred Harp singers in the Northeast. He'd been hit by polio at a young age and walked the rest of his life with a stiff limp. He had an amazing voice, sometimes singing an octave below the other basses. Comparing him to a big church organ, some people called him The Sixteen-Foot Pipe. There was no way to ignore his presence in the room: clomping on the beat, short and stumpy, fierce and unyielding.

Even the food he brought to our annual singing had a harsh, unrefined quality. He'd bring a few gallons of homemade baked beans, in a black iron Dutch oven wrapped up in a blanket to keep them hot.

To this day I sometimes call **"Cusseta"**—one of his favorites—in his honor, to keep his memory (at least for Eileen and me) alive. It's not a great tune: uncomplicated, major, no fugue or crunchy harmonies. The lyrics aren't much different than a hundred other songs.

> Show pity Lord, O Lord forgive
> Let a repenting rebel live

Every time I call "Cusseta" (though this is more and more seldom as fewer people remember Allen now) I mention him. His face is fading from my memory. Still, I work to remember him: his sweet and salty baked beans, his dark and scowling face, his cockiness as he entered the square, his sledgehammer sound.

Well known for his erratic driving, Allen was killed in a highway accident. Head-on, instant death. Only a few years before, he'd cracked up a car on the way to the Sacred Harp convention in New Jersey.

Though none of my ancestors were slaves and none of Allen's worked in Scottish coal mines, I think of him as one of my forebears. And the longer I sing the shaped notes, the clearer it is that our ancestors—biological or imaginal—come to us in rites of public music.

About fifteen singers drove to the funeral home in a little town north of Syracuse. Standing around the parking lot, before Allen's service, I felt old beyond my years. I understood a little better why one goes long distances for funerals. Guys in suits. Women dressed up. All of them holding their *Sacred Harps*.

Somebody had searched through the minutes books and found out which tunes Allen had sung the most in his last few years. We all had a different sense of what his favorites were, but we also all agreed that his leading style was uniquely his own: clomping into the middle of the square with his polio-stricken leg, choosing a song and then tossing his book aside, groan-singing "two three four" to mark the rests between verses.

The experience of singing at his funeral was the closest I've ever come to the ancient practice of keening, pouring out grief through loud, untrammeled song. I saw more tears at this funeral than at any I'd been to before. Allen's sons were overcome with loss: so much unfinished business, so sudden. A dozen people they'd never met, wailing out their lamentation.

We were on the road for a while when Eileen realized she'd left her *Sacred Harp* behind. Though easily replaceable—we had a box of books at our house—it was obvious we had to turn around and go back to the funeral home. The book was still there, waiting for her.

WEEPING PILGRIM

I met Allen Fannin at the first all day singing I attended in the north. During a magical break in our grinding winter, I drove three hours to Binghamton to sit in the hollow square with fifty others drawn from ten New York State counties. A short time into the six-hour singing, a girl of perhaps ten years heard her name called and got up to lead. A hundred eyes were on her, and fifty loud and rowdy voices rose as she brought her arm down and launched us into her first pick. "I'm a poor, mourning pilgrim. I'm bound for Canaan's land."

George Pullen Jackson describes children leading at a 1930 Texas Sacred Harp Convention this way: "At first the happy children received merely a warm handshake and pat on the shoulder... But by degrees the wave of emotion rose, swept on by this song and then by another spliced on ... until the warm congratulatory reception became a veritable and ardent love feast ... smothered by kisses ... tears streamed down the cheeks ... crying, laughing, sweating ..."

There were no tears and kisses when this northern

child sat down after leading, but I saw a trace of that joy which Jackson had witnessed.

It must have been terrifying for her. Many adults won't stand in the center to lead. There are expectations, traditions, a right and wrong way to do it. But much more daunting is the din of dozens of human voices slamming into you from all four sides. Swept into the burgeoning flood of sound, the inexperienced leader is like a bit of flotsam in a rising floodtide.

Some wait years to get up their nerve and lead. It's not unheard of for people to practice in a full-length mirror before standing in front of a large group. Laura tricked Eileen the first time, saying "Come on, we'll lead together." They got up and started in. Laura eased back and by the time the song was over, Eileen was alone in the middle. She never needed encouragement to lead again.

Yet this ten-year-old got right up and led with the combination of poise and awkwardness that makes girls of her age so charming. She wanted to be grown up, part of the group, accepted and good at it. Yet she still wanted to be a kid, looking to the adults for guidance. While leading, she kept her eyes on the front row tenors, following the up and down pump of their arms, very deliberate, entirely focused.

She chose hard tunes. Her first was "Weeping Pilgrim," with a $\frac{2}{4}$ to $\frac{3}{4}$ meter switch between verse and chorus, that many adults won't attempt. The other was "Messiah," which was unfamiliar to many that day.

> He comes, He comes, to judge the world,
> Aloud th' archangel cries,

> While thunders roll from pole to pole,
> And lightning cleave the skies;
> Th' affrighted nations hear the sound,
> And upward lift their eyes.
> The slumb'ring tenants of the ground
> In living armies rise.

She seemed so somber and serious while leading. But done, she sat down and her face was lit by a huge bright smile. Relief perhaps, to have done it: still a kid—watched over—but clearly accepted and even cherished by the adults.

Later, watching her sing in the front row of the trebles was almost as delightful for me. She seemed so abandoned, truly letting the passionate sound rip. The New York State trebles were good that day: a loud silvery crest riding across the top of the surging chords. It was uncanny to see a preteen girl sing so freely, her mouth cranked wide open, eyes clenched shut. Just at the age when all the other kids are learning to hide behind their sullen coolness, their walls of faked indifference, she was free.

In some ways she was a perfect image of what I longed for. Open, unafraid, passionate, and yet not just a crazy loose cannon. She was free and at the same time she was also part of something larger than her own whims. In contrast, I'd done numerous nights on grimy stages, bellowing mad lyrics, filling my sax with screams or banging on a beat-up guitar, venting my rage. Right before I attended my first big singing, I'd bought a slick new guitar amp. Cranked up in my basement, it produced a numbing squall.

But a few days after being pummeled by the loudest

human voices I'd ever heard, swamped in the steaming gospel stew, I decided I didn't need props anymore. I returned the amp, got my money back and haven't touched an electric guitar since.

After sitting next to him at that first big sing in Binghamton, I became friends with an old guy named Ron. Over the years, he kidded me a lot, calling me "Son," and putting his arm around my shoulder when we sang about "enemies from hell." His favorite tune was "The Better Land." The last time I saw him, he called that one, got up to lead, and kept exhorting the group to go faster and faster. His body, wracked by illness and old age, couldn't keep up with his hunger for more speed. So, I left the front bench and joined him in the center, pumping my arm to keep up the desired momentum. He collapsed at a sing not long after that and had to be taken directly to the hospital. I never saw him again.

MEMORIAL LESSON #1

We sing with the dead and we sing for the dead. We join our voices with those who've gone before, and we raise our voices to keep memory alive.

At every Sacred Harp convention, there comes a time for what is called The Memorial Lesson. This usually involves a brief talk about mortality—thinking about those who've died in the last year. Then comes the reading of the names and a song for those not with us that day.

I've experienced memorial lessons that are perfunctory: a nod in the direction of Deep South tradition. I've also sat in a room where tears flowed and the quiet (especially sandwiched between many hours of blisteringly loud hymns) was almost unearthly. Traditionally, these memorial lessons were for singers, but in the last few decades, names of loved ones known only to individual singers are read too.

Most moving are the moments when a singer who'd been a regular is remembered. "George used to sit right there on the front bench of the basses. I can still hear his voice." George was a blowhard and a bully, but I miss him too. He could be unpleasant; nonetheless, he did a great deal to revive the tradition in the north. He also had a good strong voice. The last time I saw him was in Waterville, a small village on Federal Route 20. During lunch, George went around table to table and said goodbye. A month or two later he was dead from cancer.

Not long after that, we raised our voices at the gates of death. At the local monthly sing, one of our regulars asked us if we'd go to the nursing home and sing for her mother, who would soon be departing this world. After a very long decline, she'd had a stroke and then stopped taking food and liquids.

Nine of us went to her room, surrounded the bed, and sang four tunes: "Wondrous Love" ("When I am free from death"—oh yeah), "Amazing Grace" (which we call "New Britain"), "All is Well" and "Holy Manna." She looked like she already was dead: gray skin, gaping mouth, nothing but bones.

The next day I got a call from my voice teacher. She told me that death had come ten minutes after we'd left the room. Our friend's mother waited for her daughter to return and then let herself die. So, we were there. We ushered her into the next life. We were the last thing she experienced on earth.

At the New York State Sacred Harp Convention, we sang 168 songs in two days. Much of it was great, but one piece stood out. "Farewell Anthem" takes up three pages out of five hundred, right in the middle of the book, as I was in the middle of the sound.

I sat on the front bench of the tenors, aiming my voice into the plaintive roar. Four waves of human sound, grief and joy in equal parts, singing against the fact of death.

"My friends, I am going a long and tedious journey. Never to return." That phrase, "never to return," is repeated four times in a row, then "never never never never," followed by the cry of hope. "And God grant that we may meet together in that world above."

As chairman of the convention, I stood to give the memorial lesson. I had no prepared notes, saying merely, "Some of us might not be here next year. If I still am, I want to remember those of you who aren't." I looked around slowly, meeting gazes, nodding and breathing in the somber mood. Then I mentioned a few people who'd died years before, whose faces and voices still have a place in my memory.

I read the list for this year. One of the singers who'd died recently was a guy from New York City who I never liked. Grief for those we truly miss: this feeling is familiar. But what about calling to mind those we only tolerate, or truly dislike? I barely knew this guy, but on the rare occasions when we'd been at the same sing, he always annoyed me. He insisted on setting up a tripod and videoing the sing without asking if anyone minded. I did and I do. I hate the impulse in people to try to capture the ineffable, to make a paltry video record of genuine—and fleeting—human experience.

So, the last time I was at a sing with this guy—in New Jersey—when he wasn't looking, I turned his camera upward and he got five hours of the blank white ceiling. At the time I was amused by my prank. Now I wonder if it was more than that, perfect in fact, a glimpse of the afterlife as undifferentiated whiteness.

I didn't know he was dead until I read the list. Now he was off to that vast emptiness above, "where trouble shall cease and harmony shall abound," (as we sang in "Farewell Anthem.") Who will watch the video? Probably no one. The sound still ran, so he did capture our songs of death and rebirth, doubt and assurance, loss and gain. But no faces, no bodies, no shadow.

A few days later Eileen and I sat at the kitchen table where I'm writing this book, where we've eaten our meals together for decades, side by side, and we sang through the "Farewell Anthem." Without the bass and alto parts, it wasn't so satisfying, but still, just the two of us singing, did call up the past and allowed me to peer into the future.

> Hark! Hark! my dear friends, for death hath called me,
> And I must go and lie down in the cold and silent grave,
> Where the mourners cease from mourning and the pris'ner is set free:
> Where the rich and poor are both alike.
> Fare you well my friends.

NEARER, MY GOD, TO THEE

Kester has three sons. One works in high tech, over in Huntsville. Donny does excavation with heavy equipment. The third left Sand Mountain and never returned, wanting nothing to do with Sacred Harp and his family traditions.

I only hear about this lost son by accident. Hanging up my clothes in a closet, I see the time-faded lines drawn to show the three sons' growth. "Who's Howland?" I ask. Silence, broad and deep, falls on the little group that's gathered for more informal music after the big sing.

Kester's family has another book. This is a homemade collection: xeroxes of tunes that you won't find in *The Sacred Harp*. The covers are plain black and the pages are held together with brass clips. Here are the sentimental songs that people usually think of when they hear the term *southern gospel*. "Love at Home," "Farther Along," "Precious Memories," "The Sweet By and By," "The Old Rugged Cross." Sitting on the porch or around the kitchen table, Kester's cousins will sing these, not the hard and heavy hymns of dread. This was also where I learned (by accident) that southern ladies sometimes say "Bless your heart" the way northern harridans say "Go fuck yourself."

"I bet you didn't know," Kester tells me, "this was the last one they sang on the Titanic, when she was going down." He loves Lowell Mason's "Nearer My God to Thee." Did somebody sing this tune as the ship sank? Maybe. But there's no hard evidence. As far as we know, the dance band could've been doing a lively two-step or a lugubrious "God Save the King." On Kester's porch, they take "Nearer My God" very slowly, singing it as though they're holding something fragile in their hands.

Hymn-writer Lowell Mason is buried in suburban New Jersey. So, capping the Garden State Convention in Montclair, eight singers go out to pay our respects at his grave. After wandering around the hideous maze of northern Jersey for a while, our two-car procession finds the right mock-gothic entrance and makes its circuitous way to Mason's resting place. Little knolls, narrow roadways, mature trees, big stones: a very charming Victorian cemetery only a few miles from Manhattan.

After a bit of standing around in silence, we hand out the xeroxes. Our four-part rendition of **"Nearer, My God, to Thee,"** there at his grave, is quiet and calm and almost devout.

It feels great to be there in such a beautiful place, remembering somebody who'd done a good thing by writing such a charming song. I don't have any delusions that anyone will ever sing at my grave. It's unlikely that I'll even have a gravestone. Still, it did my heart good to know that a few people understand what it means to honor the dead.

Our time at Mason's grave involves no technology except the shape notes. No pictures, no recording of the event other than in these words. Just eight people and countless silent stones. Standing there it feels like I've escaped the sheer physical ugliness of modern culture for a few minutes, gone to a place where rest and respect for the old ways is not only acceptable, but exactly right. We give a blessing through the song, and in his way, Mason gives the blessing back.

In certain shaped note circles, Lowell Mason is execrated, for supposedly purging the old song books of the loud-fast-exuberant fuguing tunes. Allied with the Better Music Movement, he's presumed to have made sure that the rough democratic sound was expunged from American hymnody.

So, as our parting shot, we sing **"Northfield,"** knowing that Mason hated the speed, the energy, the rawness of fuguing tunes such as this one.

We form a ragged square and let rip. I'm standing right on top of Mason's head. Now there's a bit of postmodern irony in our singing. Yeah, we love Mason's best tunes. But he was wrong to fight against the fugues, with his arrogance and stuffy musical decorum. And we're here to let him know.

I don't have kids, so I pass this note on to my imaginary posterity: people will hold you responsible for your actions long after you're dead. We didn't piss on Mason's stone (as one of my friends is proud to say he did at the grave of Nathanial Rochester). We don't sneer and snicker. But Lowell Mason is dead and we're not. And the Yankee tune-smith fugues have not only outlived him but are flourishing again.

So, we're reverent and irreverent. We honor the dead, and we call them to account for what they've done. As the tune ends, I imagine I can hear Mason beneath us, spinning like a sanctified chicken on a high-speed rotisserie.

My grave-hunting and grave-devotion is a twisted kind of worship, not veneration for the specific family-dead, but for the immensity of all that's lost. "The past," as a very wise man once said, "is where they keep all the good stuff."

Finding and entering the spirit: that is one goal. Another: to call on the dead and give them back their voices. On one hand, they've been co-opted by New Age saps, to speak platitudes and gassy half-truths. On the other, they've been stolen by Hollywood horror movies, turned into vicious screaming corpses whose only goal is moronic gross-out.

Why do we assume that the dead are so stupid, little better than obnoxious teenagers? If you had all of eternity to work with, would you really be drawn to glow-in-the-dark skulls, black candles, and chicken blood? The dead that I care about have something valuable to offer me, not dimwit disgust. They are the loam out of which we grow, the compost of nutrients and moisture and support that our lives, our personalities, our souls perhaps, need in order to thrive.

I hear them in the stuttering scratch of the phonograph needle at the end of a 78. Perpetual round-and-round hiss, a voice hidden in the noise, a long lonesome whispering word.

They're present in the gravestone inscriptions worn to gritty oblivion. Religious rhyme, warnings and statements of faith, four-line spells, now obliterated. I run my finger in the worn grooves and feel their meaning even if my eyes cannot decipher the actual words.

I see their trace in wooden tools that have soaked up decades of sweat, black stains where a strong man yanked on this saw handle or twisted this screwdriver or swung with his calloused hands this heavy framing hammer.

I feel them in the crude prose of 19th century preachers' journals, which I've been collecting and reading for years. Stilted syntax, obscure referents, lost vocabulary, strange and unpleasant notions: they wrote of their lives in a kind of unconscious god-haze. Or so it seems reading them centuries later, not reprints but the real thing: brittle pages, split spines, misspellings, and fractured grammar.

And, most frequently, I hear the dead in the old weird country music. Honky-tonk, fiddle tunes, murder ballads, and gospel tunes with no polish or pretense.

> Broad is the road that leads to death,
> And thousands walk together there;
> But wisdom shows a narrow path,
> With here and there a traveler.

EASTER, AT SUICIDE CORNERS

I own dozens of Sacred Harp recordings: archaic and recent, professionally made and folk music documents that hiss like pit vipers. But I hardly ever listen to these CDs, cassette tapes, and old vinyl discs. Recorded shape note doesn't satisfy. Unlike so much great music, it must be experienced from the inside. The closest analogy is a vast church organ (each one of us a pipe) built into the structure of a worship space. The church itself, the people in the pews, are part of the instrument.

So when I hit the road, I seldom play shape note music. Much better for traveling are the country songs which flourished in the same steaming Baptist swamp, made by and for poor, white, shit-kickers.

Today I'm sitting behind the wheel, cruising Route 20, aiming for Suicide Corners. I'm in my own private church of speed and sound. Instead of pastel Easter Sunday greetings and "Up from the grave He arose," I've got Hank Williams wailing on "You're Getting Closer to the Grave Each Day." Alabama's favorite son, Hank was the Messiah, or at least he was what the Messiah would've looked and sounded like if he'd been born hardscrabble poor in 1923. Hank would be the Savior if Jesus had been a full-blown alcoholic by age fourteen and died drunk in the back of a behemoth Cadillac instead of on the cross.

I'm traveling the longest road in America, which in theory still goes from coast to coast (across the top of the U.S., not through the middle.) But since the building of the interstates, Old Federal Route 20 has been redone, rerouted, chopped up into mostly meaningless chunks of road in and around a hundred cities from Boston to Oregon.

Here though, three hundred miles straight east and west across New York State, Route 20 still maintains its archaic identity, if not its importance. Along its path, a few traces of the old weird country remain: abandoned cabin enclaves, a Petrified Creatures tourist trap, a great rusting teepee, faked '50s burger joints that used to be the real thing, desolate adultery motels, gas stations with porticos to pull up under in the rain, taxidermy shops, the White Horse Tavern, the Elim Bible Institute, nineteenth century prisons (Attica, Auburn), the Rolling Hills mental asylum (abandoned), a sulfur spring resort haunted by ancient Hasidim, and the Onondaga Indian reservation. In short, it's my own private lost highway.

I'm riding this sunny late springtime afternoon with Hank Williams as my yahoo yawping copilot and my spiritual guide. While alive, Hank played to the poor sentimental rubes plagued by hookworm and Jesus. He sang about broken hearts, Satan, family ties, rivers of alcohol, and salvation—gained and lost. Long dead, he sings now for me.

If you know one tune by Hank Williams, it's likely to be "I Saw the Light." The sentimental millions who want Hank to be a gooey religious sap go for that one. Then there are the fans who resonate with his lifelong romantic misery, loving "Your Cheating Heart." For me, it's his songs of doom that resonate most. Heading due west on Route 20, I listen to these tunes, digging deep into his archive of despair: "The battle of Ammy-godden," (Hank's version of "Armageddon"), "The Devil's Train," and "Lost Highway."

James Dean is probably America's favorite car crash celebrity (handsome, young, cool, fast). Ira Louvin is less celebrated, but he too gave up his life in the screech of burning rubber and brake shoes. For me, though, Hank Williams is the true patron saint of automotive doom. He spent most of his professional life traveling the Lost Highway and died in a manner perfectly befitting such a path.

Hank has no equal as America's poet of drinking, driving, the Devil, and death. He wails about the disaster area that once was his heart, the smoking bomb crater that once was his soul. Then the next cut comes out of my dashboard speakers and Hank's got a message for me about the Alabama Angel of Death. I see that specter as Hank himself, in a fake cowboy suit spangled with silvery skulls and gleaming black rhinestones. Could there be a better death angel than somebody who sprawled out in the back seat of his powder blue Cadillac, full of narcotic pills and liquor, and drifted into death-sleep while heading for his next show?

Just past Texaco Town (yes, it's on my map), I

approach Suicide Corners (also a real place). I know this spot by reputation and memory, having almost died here decades ago, when Eileen tried to pass a truck on this blind stretch of rural nowhere. We were in her first car, a 1965 Impala. A hard-smoking great aunt from Florida had given her the car after having it repainted battleship gray. In this, our Motor City dreadnought, we were heading toward Canada when a semi appeared like the great iron fist of a very angry God. We veered, air horns blasted, and the Angel of Death had to wait for another chance to claim me.

Legendary for decades, Suicide Corners is the perfect spot to get yourself a killer car accident. Now it's all lit up with flashers on pylons and frantic warning signs. And still, by virtue of a strange combination of dips and rises, and bad karma, it provides plenty of opportunities to get pulverized in a broadside crash.

I slow down, feeling the chilly Motor City deathvibe. I get off Route 20 here, but stop after a short distance and turn around, to face the deadly intersection from the north. Passing through, I make another backtrack. From this angle too, oncoming trucks would be unseen, if not unheard. One more stop, a reverse and a return. Thus, I approach Suicide Corners from all four directions, making my automotive sign of the cross.

In old Hoodoo rites, the desolate crossroads was the best place to slit a chicken's throat and make your deal with strong dark gods. I'm not selling my soul today, or trading it away. All the same, it occurs to me that this would be an excellent spot to transact some dubious spiritual business.

Hank, wailing about glory and the grave, would I'm sure agree. Today he has a warning for me about the lights growing dimmer and "dark shadders" creeping on me. But he well understood that we all make deals with the Devil. And here, crisscrossing Suicide Corners, the offer is mighty hard to resist.

Hank played at being an aw shucks good ole boy, with songs so deceptively simple that they reached past the deep layer of sentimental goo that surrounds the hard, mean, weary Southern soul. Underneath that simplicity was a seething cloud of darkness. "My bucket's got a hole in it." The raw drain hole of black despair—his whole life running down and out. On first listen, it's just a complaint that he can't get no beer with his bucket. But his bucket contains his whole life and there's a hole that cannot be filled: a bottomless need in Hank's soul.

Instead of going to church on this Easter morning, I stayed home and listened to Hank—listened, sang along, and banged out the chords on Eileen's eighty-year-old piano, before getting on the road. "Six more miles to the graveyard, six more miles long and sad." There can be no better way to celebrate the entrance of King Jesus into Jerusalem on the back of a borrowed Holy Land ass.

After my mini morning Hankathon, I drive an hour west, into the wilds of redneck Old York State. Forget any fantasies of glammy Manhattan. Let go of fetid Brooklyn and Bronx. Forget skyscrapers, Broadway, Central Park, the vastness of the slumscape and over-polished gleam of millionaire mansions. This is the Other New York: a lost corner, snowbound for months at a time, tucked between two Great Lakes, Canada, and the wilds of

Pennsyltucky. As far as most Americans are concerned, it might as well be on the dark side of Mars. This is my territory: fifty thousand square miles of Somewhere Else with Route 20—my Lost Highway—running all the way through.

On this sunny Sunday, everybody is declaring that Jesus is back, after three days' harrowing Hell. At the tomb, the stone's been rolled away and the Lord is risen. And because it's Easter, all the liquor stores in my town are closed. But I'm in luck, finding on Route 20 a lonely gas station where I can pick up a 40-ounce can of malt liquor while everybody else is hunting for colored eggs and gnawing on bad, too-damn-salty ham.

Going past Suicide Corners, I journey deeper into Genesee County, with Hank and his bastard offspring, fine degenerate country music, to keep me company.

"The Old Man's Drunk Again" (Jimmy Martin)

"Too Many Pills" (Arkie Blue)

"Life in Prison" (the Merle Haggard version, then Gram Parsons)

"You'll Die a Thousand Deaths" (Ferlin Husky)

"Gotta Get Drunk" (Willie Nelson)

"Drivin' Nails in My Coffin" (Ernest Tubb)

"The Pills I Took" (Hank Williams the Third—who never knew his grandfather)

"The Kneeling Drunkard's Plea" (Johnny Cash, then the Louvin Brothers)

I am well aware that no matter how heartfelt Hank and his despondent spawn might sound, there was always an element of the bogus in their high lonesome cries. They were showmen, playing to their audience and giving them what they wanted to hear. Hank starred at the Grand Ole Opry, but Nashville is now a loathsome combination of Top 40 and Las Vegas. What passes for country music these days has all the authenticity of a Disney ride or the word "love" from the lips of a twenty-dollar street hooker. But genuine, out-of-tune, tear-sodden gospel or miserable hymns of grief: this is where my mind, my tongue, my ears, and heart are drawn.

Why such gloom on a lovely spring day, when millions of others are celebrating Christ's triumph over the grave? Why dive into the dark heart of the old weird country on Easter Sunday? Perhaps it's just that I find it difficult—often impossible—to shuffle along with the great herds of humanity. But perhaps also this little pilgrimage into Genesee County is a moving toward something, not merely a flight away or an ornery refusal.

Eventually, I pass the church with the witch-hat steeple where I'd led the singing school a while back. In the morning, the lot must've been full. Now, in bright afternoon sunshine, the place is abandoned.

Consulting my maps and listening to Hank wail about the Devil's Train (long and black, beautiful to see), I end up in Linden, a hamlet tucked into a little dell with a pretty—if inaccessible—waterfall.

There's also a house totally armored with corroded metal signs. Coke, Pepsi, Burma Shave, gear oil, Crisco, Swamp Root. In front of the house, standing sentry, is a human-sized rabbit propped up on an ancient motorcycle (more rust than iron, more dust than rubber.)

Linden, I now realize, is the far end of my Easter pilgrimage: the secret crazed death village I was told ab

Th. Metzg

after our singing school. This is where, once upon a time, the famously mysterious Linden Murders took place. The guy who'd organized the singing school at his witch-hat church had taken me aside afterward and told me all he knew about the crimes. Three times, over the course of a decade, the same killer struck—literally. All his victims had their faces bashed in. Horrible, now forgotten, never solved.

I don't see a single person in Linden. I wouldn't call it a ghost town, but on that mild, bright afternoon, all of Linden's residents are invisible.

BATTLEGROUNDS OF MEMORY

We flew down to Atlanta and stayed with a guy we hardly knew. He'd been to Rochester once, to visit friends from college, and had come the first time we held the New York State convention in our town. Others too had made the trek to western New York State when we hosted the convention. We'd gone all the way to their sings (in Virginia, Massachusetts and Philadelphia) and it was common courtesy to return the visit when we held our big event.

In Atlanta, our accommodations were hardly deluxe, but that was irrelevant. I'd gotten sick on the flight down, a nasty airplane cold, and so went the whole weekend in a blur of fever and sore throat. I drank a lot of scalding black coffee and told myself, "I'm here, I'm going to sing, I'll pay the price when I get home."

Much of that trip is gone from memory, though I do recall that the best part wasn't the singings. They were fine and the people were welcoming enough. One all-day was in a beautiful, nineteenth century country church packed to the doors. Another, in an Atlanta suburb, was maybe a dozen-and-a-half people, in a bland modern church foyer. By then my throat was raw and red. I switched over to sing treble, sitting next to a guy from Texas. I enjoyed that for an hour or two, hanging up above the harmonies, making a sound that was half high lonesome and half moon-drunk hoot owl.

The best part of the trip was when our host took us to Oakland Cemetery to visit the grave of B. F. White, the compiler of the original *Sacred Harp*. There's a tintype from the 1870s of White and his wife Thurza (née Golightly) that makes them seem not just far off in time, but much more foreign than my German and Scottish ancestors. Wearing what looks like a clerical collar, White might be a Puritan divine from the 1600s. Hard and sour, he's clearly not a man who suffered fools or enemies gladly. The image is seen on T-shirts now at singings, with a fatuous slogan ("The best sings in life are free") under the grim old southern faces. There's nothing "best" or "free" about either of them, as far as I can tell.

Our host in Atlanta thought we'd want to see their grave, and he was right. We didn't sing there, though I'm sure others have done some tunes right there on top of his moldering bones. Cemetery memorial sings are a long tradition—when people go to brighten up the graves with flowers and song. We heard that there's a plot somewhere in the South with the stones arranged in four parts, in a hollow square, tenors facing altos, basses facing the trebles. Mythic burying ground or just poetic fancy, I liked the idea of people laid out in death the way they'd spent their best days alive.

Not far from White's grave is the final resting place

of Margaret Mitchell, author of *Gone with the Wind*. Though I love Hollywood of that era, and though Vivien Leigh was then gorgeous, I hated the movie. The book was even worse; I didn't get past the first chapter. I was respectful at her graveside, though I felt nothing but disdain for Mitchell, whose claim to literary glory is a vapid nine-hundred-page soap opera.

The Old South, nonetheless, held a fascination for me long before I sang a single tune from *The Sacred Harp*. The most important class I ever took in college was a semester-long journey into the work of William Faulkner. Taught with passion and brilliance by Clay Lewis, it was my first real dive into the alien world of the Deep South. Clay had grown up there; three of his four great-grandfathers had been in the Confederate Army. Clay had been an officer in the Marine Corps and had ended up teaching in western New York State, firmly in Yankee country, because of blind academic luck. From him, and his love of Faulkner's novels, I got my baptism into southern gothic, with its self-destructive macho violence, pervasive reek of doom, and soul-gnawing guilt.

Clay said that the small college town of Geneseo, where our paths crossed, was a lot like Faulkner's Mississippi. There was a rich family (the Wadsworths) which owned huge swaths of land all around Geneseo, and which sent sons off to become congressmen and generals. There were two branches of this ruling family, and two sprawling estates, one at either end of Main Street. The mansions were far enough back that I could only get a glimpse of their decaying glory. Instead of freed slaves, Livingston County had shantytowns full of Italian immigrants, who labored in the farm fields and descended into the largest salt mine in the Western Hemisphere. The college campus had a fine view of the valley, broad and sleepy, with frequent lurid sunsets. Far off to the West was the tiny specter of the original mine head, still the tallest structure in Livingston County.

My first semester at Geneseo, I dove deep into the gorgeous literary nightmare that is Faulkner's South. His prose had power such as I'd never encountered before. There's hardly any singing or instrumental music in his novels. Yet the language itself, when Faulkner got out of his own way and let himself go, still reverberates inside my skull. Some of the sentences make little sense, yet they ring in my memory, a kind of song made purely of language. Taken all together, the books make up a vast, sprawling Christ-haunted murder ballad.

This was no smug Yankee caricature, but the vision of a writer who lived his entire life deep in the heart of Dixie: replete with barely concealed incestuous desire, the ruins of the Lost Cause, rage, and blood lust. Faulkner's cast of characters was a parade of the grotesque: Popeye the rapist, Benjy the prophet who can barely speak, Percy Grimm the wannabe stormtrooper, Miss Emily who sleeps with her dead lover, boot-legging thugs, blood-mad Baptists, con men, and world-weary whores. The novel that stood out above them all, conquering my mind, was *Absalom, Absalom*: a seething, overwrought beast of a book with prose so convoluted and obsessional that the reader must either give in and abjectly submit, or close the cover and flee for safety.

Years later, I understood Faulkner's grief in a new

way, pouring myself into "David's Lamentation," which some say is the most beautiful song in *The Sacred Harp*. In the chorus, King David weeps and cries out, "O my son! Would to God I had died for thee Absalom, my son, my son."

I make no apologies for my bibliolatry. Books did it; I entered first through the printed page. Only then, book-besotted, could I open myself to the sound, the smell, and taste of the Deep South. Only after I had allowed myself to be swamped by verbiage could I sojourn in actual bodily form to sun-scorched, red-dirt Alabama.

Clay moved out of the area and I stayed. He worked for twenty-five years on his memoir of growing up in the south. It was published the year I discovered Sacred Harp. He sent me a copy of the book, *Battlegrounds of Memory*, and I understood more fully why Faulkner was so important for him. All that blind suffering, so much refusal, aloneness, and silence. His mother had seen a lynching—a whole family hanged—and his description of being taken to that tree as a boy matches for guilt and horror anything in Faulkner's body of work.

SECESSION

A guy I'd never seen before got up to lead, and announced to the group that he was there representing the "Free State of Winston." I heard a few uncomfortable laughs and saw some embarrassed scowls. During our break for dinner on the grounds, I asked Kester about it, and he shrugged it off. "He's from Winston County. That's all."

Actually there was a lot more to it than that. Before we took off that day, I found the Free State guy and he told me that Winston County, Alabama, had never seceded from the Union. While most of the South rallied to the Confederate flag, the people of Winston said *no*, and voted to secede from Alabama. The reason was simple: because of the county's rugged terrain—hills, gorges, poor soil—there was almost no cotton planting, and thus few slaves, in Winston. As more than one honest Southerner has said, secession brought on "a rich man's war and a poor man's fight."

At the sing the rigid smiles and pro forma politeness didn't hide others' discomfort. This guy was talking to a Yankee about something most Alabamans would prefer to forget. We drifted away from the church so that he could speak freely.

In the first months after secession, in the heart of Dixie, Winston Unionists formed home guard units to defend themselves against the Confederacy. At a conclave held at Looney's Tavern, near the town of Addison, a resolution was passed that declared those present would refuse to fight the Union and the Confederacy and requested to be left alone by both sides to "work out our own political and financial destiny."

The governor responded by issuing writs of arrest for those in the county who were guilty of so-called treason against the Confederacy and also demanding the resignations of militia commanders who would not take the oath of office. In 1862, the hill-country Unionists faced a Confederate draft, and many fled into the county's wild forests and rugged canyons to avoid Confederate raiders who forayed into Winston to seize so-called deserters and draft-dodgers. A few of the county's residents served the Union by helping loyalists escape to the safety of Union lines.

In short, quite a few Alabamans wanted nothing to do with the slaveholders' rebellion. But the years passed, and the South's sentimentalized Lost Cause became enshrined in revisionist popular fiction such as *The Klansman*, and the film that was based on it, *The Birth of a Nation*.

Not only were there violent acts of retribution during and following the war, but for decades afterward the state of Alabama continued to punish the people of Winston. This, and not the backward ways of the

Winstonites, explains why paved roads, telephone service, and electrification lagged far behind other counties that had sent their men off to battle against the U.S.

Driving back to Kester's farm, I'd gotten a good look at the burnt-out remains of a barn. I must have noticed that his attention was drawn to the ruin as we went slowly past, so I asked what had happened there. Kester was matter of fact. "My second cousin burned it down." Asked why, he didn't seem the least bit perturbed. "Just plain plumb meanness." When I told this to another guy, he said, "God'll get even with 'em. That's what we call Alabama karma."

Back home, where I had access to good libraries, I did some more poking around in the Winston story. I found out that the people of that county weren't the only ones who said *no* to the Confederacy. A map of Alabama made the situation clear. When the state seceded, three counties voted 90 to a 100 percent cooperation with the Union. Eight others voted 70 to 90 percent to refuse participation in the slaveholders' rebellion. All of the counties were in the north of Alabama, where the soil and geography made cotton planting futile. In other words, the Alabamans who didn't have slaves didn't see any reason to fight against the legitimate government of the U.S.

GENUINE

When I came to Sacred Harp, I had the pig-headed puritanical notion that there was such a thing as pristine American folk music. Not patriotic, but definitely ethnocentric, I was convinced that I'd found a music suffused with authenticity.

Laura, the Den Mother of our local group, said that watching Eileen and me absorb *The Sacred Harp* was like something out of a science fiction movie. After our first big sing, we were transformed, sucking in the sound like aliens sucking in human life force. In those early days, I was convinced that these tunes were somehow more authentic, more *real*, than all the other hymns I'd ever sung. Opening the book was like striking a vein of pure American folk-gold.

I paged reverently through the tattered original songbooks that Laura collected, peering into the past. Note for note most of the songs had not been altered. I loved the idea that our singing was how it had sounded two hundred years back. The harmonies were largely untouched. The lyrics had been left alone, for the most part.

And we sometimes sang in buildings as old as the songs. These were epitaphs brought to life—the spirit of the old lost America resurrected.

However, the deeper I went, the more I learned, the more this notion was in peril. I found out that "Wondrous Love" was based on a British street ballad celebrating Captain Kidd the pirate. There were fiddle tunes in the book, harmonized and *evangelized* (given Christian lyrics.) Nothing wrong with that, I told myself. It was still folk music. Less palatable were two songs attributed to Ignaz Pleyel, a student of Haydn. "Home, Sweet Home" is called by some the most popular American song of the nineteenth century. It appears in *The Sacred Harp* as "Sweet Home," a rather tepid tune that seldom gets called in the north. A little harder to swallow was a German drinking song I learned from my father. "Ja, Ja, Ja, Ja!"

Far more popular, at least in northern sings, was **"O Come Away."** It's a genuine (whatever that means) temperance song.

> Come hail the day that celebrates
> The ransom of the inebriates.

After welcoming the repentant boozer to the fold, the song goes on to brag about rescuing men **"from a drunkard's grave."** I took great pleasure in hammering with my voice on the words **"We welcome you here, ye who with taste** *perverted*..." The tune wraps up with an exhortation to "come sign the pledge!" In other words, to publicly foreswear ever taking another drop of demon rum.

At northern sings, this is all a big joke. People sing it in a slurred soused voice, purposely out of tune and out of time. At the end there's always a laugh and a few shouts of "Prost!" "Salud!" and "L'chaim!" In the South, however, the song is still held in reverence.

My favorite experience of **"O Come Away"** was singing it in an eighteenth-century tavern. This was at the Farmer's Museum in Cooperstown. Here, the past had been lovingly preserved. Buildings slated for destruction were transplanted, and as in other such mock villages where we sang, it was possible to pretend I'd gone back in time. Strolling the lanes, I could see butter churned, a blacksmith banging on tongues of red-hot iron, barrels made, and pages of type set letter by letter.

Someone had organized a big sing for the museum village. Though we didn't dress up in period costumes, we were to be a taste of the past for visitors. All I recall of that day happened beyond the hollow square. At the end, someone yelled out that we should all repair to the delightfully named Bump Tavern (raised in 1795) and there to make the rafters ring. Real beer was served as we gave a rousing rendition of **"O Come Away!"**

I enjoyed another jape that day, a flat-out hoax. The Farmer's Museum is now the permanent home of the Cardiff Giant. One of America's greatest flimflams, the giant is a ten-foot-tall stone man found underground in 1869. He'd been secretly carved in Iowa and shipped to New York State as a way for the perpetrator to thumb his atheist nose at so-called biblical inerrancy. "There were giants in those days." So saith Genesis VI: 4. And thus the 2,990 pound giant was created, hidden and unearthed. Within weeks, thousands had paid to see the putative petrified man.

He was bought by a syndicate, moved to a better location, and continued to draw hordes of both the credulous and the scoffers. P. T. Barnum offered $50,000 to buy the Prehistoric Giant. When he was turned down, he had a plaster cast surreptitiously made and displayed his giant at his museum, claiming it was the genuine article and that the real hoax was a counterfeit.

After singing **"O Come Away"** in the tavern, I went to pay my respects to the giant. The museum displayed him then in a pit, six feet down, reburied and partially uncovered to recreate the original fakery. The crowd was much smaller than in his glory days. But the giant was still much admired, and not just because of his flaccid, yet still mammoth, circumcised manhood. He'd been carved in an awkward, twisted position, and seemed to be writhing in embarrassment down there naked in the dirt. I heard later that he'd been exhumed and moved (for the fifth, sixth, seventh time?) to a place more proper to a museum exhibit: well lit, dry and secure. I prefer to remember him as I saw him: at the bottom of a bogus grave.

GOSPEL GOTHIC

Mennonites are not known for their ironic wit or edgy hipness. Yet "Ye Heedless Ones" was the favorite of a husband and wife who sang with us for a few years. Hannah came from Mennonite royalty (with plenty of Kraybills, Yoders, and Zehrs in her family tree) but she wasn't old-fashioned. She never went all the way to dying her hair asphalt black, nor did she wear flashy skull rings. Still, she and Japheth were able to enjoy the twisted humor in singing:

> Ye heedless ones, who wildly stroll,
> The grave will soon become your bed,
> Where silence reigns and vapors roll
> In solemn darkness round your head.

Every time they called that tune, either Hannah or Japheth would joke about how they enjoyed going for a wild stroll.

Yet, no matter how much some people try to smirk past the truth, or avoid it with laughter, there's a deep black fatalistic vein that runs through *The Sacred Harp*. Judgement Day is no comic book fantasy. "To bear the dreadful curse"—there's no subtlety in that. "Learn from me your certain doom"—it's hard to pretty-up that one. This is gothic, not goth: the real hardcore American doom.

In the German and British gothic traditions, there are ancient castles holding horrible secrets of the past. In America, it's the church that contains the awful truth: to be saved you must have a heart that's sprinkled with Christ's blood. It's not a long leap from **"The Converted Thief"** (**"I see thee bathed in sweat and tears and welt'ring in thy blood"**) to the wolfman films I loved as a kid. Sprouting fur and fangs, skulking in the shadows, he's helpless when the transformation begins. Hearing the old harmonies and the grisly lyrics (**"fainting pangs and bloody sweat"**) I'm helpless too, pulled into the doom-dark tide.

I've seen black leather jackets, iridescent nail polish, and midnight blue mascara at sings, but there's no need for hipster Halloween costumes when some of the best songs are, as our friend Laura says, "dripping with drear."

"The Christian Warfare," makes reference to defeating Apollyon. Some new singers ask about this personage from the Book of Revelation and I tell them the truth, quoting chapter and verse. "And they had a king over them, which is the Angel of the Bottomless Pit, and his name was Apollyon, which means The Destroyer." A few verses before that there are locusts with the faces of men, the hair of women, teeth like lions', and the tails of scorpions. "And the sound of their wings was as the sound of chariots running into battle."

There's cosmic combat, but much more simple mortality. In the book are five hymns with titles about as subtle as a freshly dug grave:

> "The Dying Boy"
> "The Dying Californian"
> "The Dying Minister"
> "The Dying Christian"
> "The Dying Friend"

Searching through the book at our local sing, somebody called a tune that none of us knew: "Thou Art Passing Away." We got to the end of the first line and the whole group couldn't help but crack up.

> Thy forehead is pale, and thy pulses are low,
> And thy once blooming cheek wears an ominous glow.

This could be Edgar Allan Poe on a bad day, mooning over a beloved sickly girl-bride. Our laughter was spontaneous. "Ominous glow," somebody said, "You can't get away with that in a hymn these days. Sounds like she has radiation poisoning."

It took a minute to regroup, shake off the giggles, and start over. We got our smug smiles under control and made it to the end.

> And now in thine eye shines the fond parting tear.

149 WATTS

More than any poet, Isaac Watts gave *The Sacred Harp* its tongue. Out of nearly six hundred songs in the book, one hundred and forty-nine have words by Watts. Now mocked as hopelessly old fashioned, or shunned for his harsh theology, Watts nonetheless still speaks across the centuries. For me and Eileen, his words still have power. There is a glow—a mystic light—in his language.

From the vine:

> Our hearts are cheered with gen'rous wine
> With inward joy our faces shine.

From fire:

> As sparks fly out from burning coals
> And still are upward borne.

In heaven:

> Arrayed in robes of light
> And rays of majesty around.

And on earth:

> But when the gospel comes,
> It spreads diviner light,
> It calls dead sinners from the tombs,
> And gives the blind their sight.

Of course, Watts was not the first or last to use light in his hymns. But it's a long way from "This Little Light of Mine" to:

> Our spirits shake their eager wings,
> And burn to meet Thy flying throne;
> We rise away from mortal things,
> T'attend Thy shining chariot down.

I'll never be able to prove it. Still, I'm convinced that the missing link between Isaac Watts' mystic incandescence and Hank Williams' saving light is the 1929 phonograph record of Bascom Lamar Lunsford's "Dry Bones." The song tells the whole story of the Bible in five verses, though out of order. "Old Enoch, who lived 365 years," Paul, Moses, Ezekial ("Dry bones in that valley, got up and took a little walk around"), and finishing at the beginning, with Adam. But it's the chorus that pushed back the shadows in Hank's childhood heart.

> I saw, I saw the light from heaven
> Shining all around.
> I saw the light come shining.
> I saw the light come down.

Hank never gazed on a picture of Lunsford. But if he had, he'd have faced no fake hillbilly, with blacked out teeth and an aw-shucks grin. Lunsford wore a natty suit and bow tie when he performed. He sang North Carolina mountain songs and played banjo. Yet he was dead set against the illiterate hick image that was grafted onto the music.

Did he see the light of heaven coming down? Probably that's no more likely than Ezekial preaching to the valley of dry bones, his voice putting flesh on the skeletons, and breathing life into them.

Hank must have known that song, and probably its black gospel twin, "Dem Bones," with its jaunty chorus of "Dem bones, dem bones, gonna rise again." And though he wasn't immersed in scripture, as were so many boys of his generation, dragged to church to be harangued by sweat-reeking preachers, he did sometimes go poking through a pile of Bible bones. He knew about Samson, who fought the Philistines and was mighty, after the slaughter declaring, "With the jawbone of an ass, heaps upon heaps, with the jaw of an ass I have slain a thousand men." And Hank knew the names of the hill where Jesus was nailed to the shameful tree: Golgotha or Calvary, which means place of the skull.

A THOUSAND CORONERS

I got a call from somebody representing the American Academy of Forensic Sciences. Their annual convention was to be in Atlanta this year and they wanted me to come and speak. Besides the endless scientific papers and presentations, the convention often had a paid speaker, someone, if not light weight, at least more entertaining than another report on new models of DNA analysis.

Atlanta was the home base of Coca-Cola. The AAFS people contacted them, asking if they could provide somebody who'd speak about Coke's dark and cocaine-laced past. The calls weren't returned, so they went hunting and found me. I'm neither a coroner nor a forensic scientist, but I had published an article called "Who Put the Coke in Coca-Cola?"

I considered the offer briefly: a fat double stipend (and truth can now be told: the check came twice and I cashed them both), airfare and a stay at an absurdly posh hotel. These were attractive. But before I said yes, I went into the living room and pulled off the shelf my yearly Sacred Harp minutes book, which lists every convention and all-day sing, and every song led at these gatherings. The minutes have been kept—name of leader, number of song—going back to the 1800s. Upcoming sings are also listed.

Jackpot: the AAFS convention would be held on the same weekend as a couple of sings on Sand Mountain (only ninety miles away), I said yes. The lady asked if I needed any special tech assistance. "Just a mic that works." A month later Eileen and I flew to Atlanta.

I learned a great deal at the convention. Best of all was the knowledge that if you're fairly presentable, you can wander around a professional conference in the fanciest hotel in town, eat a lot of smoked salmon and baby asparagus and no one seems to mind. I didn't have a suit or tie. I didn't wear an ID badge, and no one stopped me from entering even the most esoteric of meetings.

At the "Britain's Most Prolific Serial Killer" autopsy breakfast, I watched a few hundred scientists snarfing down bacon and sausage while huge slides of decomposing corpses were flashed on the screen. I managed to keep the Marriot's fine food down, but after ten minutes of a scientist discussing the differences between "brain paste" and "brain sludge," I had to move on.

Other presentations included a new method of photographing corpses. Slide after slide of grayish, oozy tissue were paraded before my uncomprehending eyes. But the experts gathered for this one couldn't get enough. I wasn't able to make it for "A Deadly Mixture of Hairspray and Acetaminophen," but from the reports I got, it was a big hit with the crowd.

Go to an ordinary professional conference and you're

likely to find a vendor's room. Usually, these have a tiresome sameness. But at the AAFS's meeting, every booth held a glimpse of the grotesque. The Supercut brochure announces proudly: "Need autopsy blades? Buy the best!" Beside salesmen hawking complete solutions for human identity testing, evidence-storage shrink-wrap, and blood-spatter trajectory strings, there were lots of free gifts.

I snagged a nifty Forensic Scientist Calendar. For every month, there are charming pictures of dead people, tissue samples, and bugs infesting submerged corpses. I got some toe-tags (which I knew would be perfect on Christmas presents), evidence bags, and a genetic identification key ring.

The seminar that made the biggest impression on me, though not literally, was about Human Bite-marks. This turned out to be another slide extravaganza, with endless blurry images blown up to the size of billboards. Yes, even an amateur such as I could see the indentations of the canines and incisors.

Punchy from all the gore and goo, I stood in line during the question and answer period. After waiting through some tiresome technical queries, I got my chance to ask what part of the human body was considered the best part to eat.

The presenter hadn't been focusing on cannibalism. And he was a bit put off by my question. But he was a professional, and I didn't look like a crazed intruder off the street. So, he replied as one colleague to another.

"I'm focusing more today on human bites as aggression. Not really as ... that's not my area of research."

"But what parts of the body do you usually find are bitten off?"

The other forensic scientists were getting a bit antsy. Every word out of my mouth made it clearer I was not one of them.

"I'm sorry but I can't answer that today. I'm focusing more on—"

"Are humans white meat or dark meat?"

I heard a muttering and rumbling around me. Any minute now the Marriot's security goons would be there in force, asking for my ID.

"Thanks a lot," I said. "Great presentation." I tried to sound upbeat and professional. A look of gratitude suffused his face as I passed the mike to the next questioner.

As soon as my hour-long presentation was done, we had the valet parking guy put our bags in the trunk of the rental car and journeyed out to Sand Mountain. In two hours, we went from the fanciest hotel I'd ever stayed at to a church up on rocks, with no running water or screens on the windows.

For a couple of days, we ate a lot of BBQ, sang with some of the folks we'd gotten to know on earlier trips, and went home with a bag full of coroner swag. Best was the cute Identigene five-inch white sperm. Wind up the little crank and it slithers across the floor, with a big smile on its bulbous face. About the size of a toddler's fist, the spring-driven sperm wriggles its highly motile tail and announces that Identigene is your best bet for DNA typing supplies. An especially charming touch is the Have a Nice Day smile on his gleaming white head.

The best part of the trip wasn't the coroners'

convention or the singing, but when we stopped at Hellmore's Real Barbecue, outside of Boaz, Alabama. We'd passed a dozen other barbecue joints that day, but this one had the most perfect sign I'd ever seen. Hand-painted, perhaps ten feet by six, it loomed above the roadside. Why perfect? Because in one picture, the entire mystery of long pig (aka: the Other White Meat), cannibalism, and genuine Southern hospitality was eerily evoked.

It showed a pig wearing a butcher's get-up and a strange leer. Of course, I'd seen other images of cartoon pigs advertising pork, and chickens in chef's caps crowing about how good the fried chicken was in this place or that. As a kid I found those images disturbing. Why a smirking lobster holding knife and fork on the lobster bib? Why a happy cow with a knife and fork outside the steakhouse?

The pig at Hellmore's was of that same cannibal clan. His maniacal grin and the crimson spatters on his big shiny knife added to the fratricidal atmosphere. The drips were probably supposed to be Hellmore's All-time Champion BBQ Sauce. But they sure looked like pig blood to me. And the maniacal smile could have been something right out of a '60s-era L.S.D. exploitation film.

Inside, the place felt like a bomb shelter: unpainted cinder block walls, a stack of plastic gallon jugs in one corner of the entryway, low ceiling, and the pervasive scent of cooked flesh. The food at Hellmore's was actually quite good. They had a smoker out back, belching fragrant clouds. The coleslaw had exactly the right combination of sweet and tang. The corn bread was heavy as a brick of gold. The whole thing came on a sagging paper plate.

Though I was an obvious Yankee, the guy at the counter was fairly pleasant. Asking about the sign, however, was futile. He just shrugged his rounded shoulders. "No idea who painted it," he said. "You want extra sauce?"

We ate and then sat a while in the car, staring up at the sign. The crazed pigface captured exactly the feeling I'd have if I'd just crossed over to the twilight cannibal zone. Totally mad, thrilled and appalled at the same time. And maybe there was relief too in that crazed grin. "OK, now I've done it. OK, now I know what it feels like to eat the most mysterious of mystery meats."

ANCIENT DAYS, AGAIN

I went from Sand Mountain to Glimmerglass, expecting my head to explode. From Sacred Harp to passion-soaked opera—I thought—might put too much strain on my already over-loaded brain.

A week after getting back from Alabama, I drove a hundred-and-seventy miles due east on Route 20 to see and hear *Tosca* on the shore of Otsego Lake (AKA Glimmerglass), right down the road from where the Cardiff Giant lies in state. *Tosca* is a gorgeous tawdry mess: with its high Catholic erotic obsession, loud Te Deums, the Papal prison at Castel Sant Angelo, torture, Mariolatry, and grand suicide. And the production I saw at Glimmerglass was excellent: just the right combination of overwrought emotion and tainted religion.

The madness of opera was there from the beginning. The art form started during the Italian Renaissance as a literal revival of pagan worship. In not-so-secret rebellion against a thousand years of Christianity, a group of occult scholars in the city of Firenze concocted the first operas as their way of resurrecting Greek tragedy.

Ancient drama, esoteric ritual, classical mystery: the initiates of the Camerata saw and heard all of this on the newborn operatic stage. And to this day, fans are able to ignore the absurdities—baffling plot lines, inexplicable dance routines, and well-padded middle-aged singers pretending to be young and sexy—because the sound itself is so utterly, beautifully other.

Jumping the gap was much easier than I'd thought, even though no form of music would seem less like Sacred Harp than Italian opera. The differences are obvious and many.

Sacred Harp sings are free, whereas operas can be the most expensive music productions possible. All singers who can do four syllables—fa, so la, mi—and are willing to push their voice into the din, are welcome. True operatic singers are so unlike other humans that there's only a few thousand of them on the planet.

Elaborate costumery, aristocratic connections, gorgeous theaters, decades of training. Opera has these and Sacred Harp doesn't.

Red velvet cake, fried pie, buckets of shiny white ambrosia, fluttering funeral home fans, babies sleeping in the arms of bellowing women, moonshine, and real democracy. Sacred Harp has these and opera would dissolve into a fiery mist if any of these came near to it.

Still, there are deep, true links:

First is Orpheus. His story was told again and again on the operatic stage. At the birth of opera, no figure was more important. And though Primitive Baptists will tell you otherwise (or shake their heads sadly at such Yankee damn-foolishness), the original Sacred Harp belonged to Orpheus.

Second: duration. Operas can last for three or four hours. Big sings can go twice that long. They're called All Day for a reason.

Third: the primacy of the human voice over all other sounds.

Fourth: the irrational and all-consuming fanaticism of the devotees. Opera fanatics will stand through the night to get tickets and they will spend absurd amounts of money to obtain the best seats. Sacred Harp devotees will travel across the country, and eat way too much pig grease, if it means getting a good spot at one of the best sings.

Fifth: all those tears running out of all those eyes.

Sixth: opera has been called the Song of Love and Death. The same could be said of Sacred Harp.

Lastly and seventhly, most obscure and yet most profound, is the fact that both opera and Sacred Harp are at their deepest level pagan rites. Both are living breathing fossils, the sound and beautiful fury of ancient days.

When outsiders ask "why Sacred *Harp*?" the answer is usually a dismissive joke. "Yeah, this is heaven and we're all angels here." Or insiders with some knowledge of shape note history will make reference to the dozens of old hymn books with the word "harp" in the title. *The Columbian Harp. The Hesperian Harp. The Harp of Ages.*

More traditional singers will say that the book's title comes from the story of King David, and how he supposedly sang his Psalms accompanied by a harp. This, like so much folklore around Sacred Harp, is appealing but flatly untrue.

Yes, the lyre appears in the Old Testament. But it's the ancient Greeks, not the Hebrews, who gave us their sacred harp. It's the pagan lyre of Olympus, the instrument of Apollo, the ruler of the muses. He passed his supernatural instrument on to his son Orpheus, the greatest musician in the ancient world. With this harp, he went to hell to bring back his One True Love and then got torn to pieces by his music-mad fan-girl followers.

The lyre and the harp are not the same instrument. But at the time when Watts was composing his hymns and White was compiling *The Sacred Harp*, the terms were interchangeable. The King James Bible translated the term *kithara* (an ancient lyre that appears in both then Old and New Testaments) as "harp." Far more than the Psalms, the *Book of Revelation* shines celestial light on *The Sacred Harp*. Forget the Four Horsemen; it's the Twenty-four Elders of the Apocalypse, who "have victory over the Beast," and whose loud hymns shake the cosmos. "And I heard a voice from heaven, as the voice of many waters, and as the voice of great thunder, and I heard the voice of harpers harping on their harps."

I heard an Episcopalian choir director say that the human larynx is the real sacred harp. She also did work for the local public radio station. In her piece on my local shape note group, she told her listeners to place their hands on their throats, to hum and feel the vibrations of the human-sacred harp. Much as I like the image—attributing holy power to the vocal cords—this is a late add to the tradition, a modern rereading of the harp.

I, on the other hand, suspect that the real Sacred Harp is the lyre of the night sky, the constellation Lyra, which contains Vega, the brightest summer star. There are a few hints, a few vestigial remains of ancient astronomy. "Enfield," though not a popular tune, makes the most obvious connection, calling on the "tuneful lyre" to wake each "charming string."

> Awake and let thy flowing strains
> Glide through the midnight air,
> While high amidst the silent orb,
> The silver Moon rolls clear.

What other Christian hymn book contains a song such as "The Last Words of Copernicus"? In this tune, we address our voices to the pagan sun, "thou refulgent orb of day," and to the mysterious moon, "pale empress of the night." We sing of "sublunary bliss" and give praise to the night sky, where "sun and moon and planets roll, and stars glow from pole to pole."

Elsewhere, there is an exhortation to turn our gazes skyward, to "the third heaven where God resides." And "Christmas Anthem" explicitly makes the connection between harps and the Heavenly Hosts.

> In glory, with celestial arts,
> Angelic armies tune their harps,
> And raptured seraphs play their parts

After a day of superabundant song, too much food and too many people, I stood alone at Kester's place, staring up at the night sky. His quiet acres stretched off in all directions. In this silence, I understood the meaning of Sacred Harp's tumult. The constellations that loomed above me were not forgotten gods and mythical beasts; constellations are melodies inscribed on unseen celestial staves.

The great Elizabethan magus, John Dee, saw the world as a lyre. The structure of all creation, harmonies and dissonances, sympathies, and antipathies, is made manifest in the sounds drawn from the individual strings of this cosmic harp. This concept—the world as musical instrument—is fundamental to much of Renaissance magical thought.

Friedrich Nietzsche was born the same year as the original *Sacred Harp* was published. Though utterly ignorant of the crude, boisterous, democratic music flourishing in America, he might have been describing shaped note instead of opera in his first book. *The Birth of Tragedy from the Spirit of Music* is about staged music drama, the supposed European return of ancient Greek religious energies. Nietzsche was convinced that he was living in a time when, as in the days of tragedy in ancient Greece, myth would be reborn from the spirit of music. All that was needed was recognition and surrender, since "in the presence of music we behave as the Greeks behaved in the presence of their symbolic myths." In his day, Nietzsche proclaimed, music "generated myth once again for us."

For him, the first true operatic hero is a satyr—a sensual demon whose realm is music. Nietzsche claimed as opera's progenitor the god who challenges and darkens the sun of Apollo: Dionysus, whose ecstatic mysteries give birth to a contagious madness. Dionysus is the master of the grape harvest, winemaking, and wine. He's the wild god of rapture, life-force, ecstasy, and orgiastic communion.

None of this, of course, is mentioned, let alone discussed, at a Sacred Harp gathering. Anything that smacks of paganism is either blasphemy or an embarrassment. Still, without Apollo and Orpheus, there's no harp and no interplay of heavenly order and infernal chaos. Without the Greeks' shiny sky-god and his proto-rock-star son, there's no Sacred Harp.

PURE AND IMPURE

One of the first Sacred Harp CDs I got a hold of is called *In Sweetest Union Join*. And I have experienced moments of true blissful oneness with others in the hollow square. Strangers and old friends, young bucks and old geezers, beautiful trebles, and hard-edged altos, the good, the bad, and the painfully loud: I have joined them in times of sweet pagan bliss.

Like theater and other musical performances, it's expected that we gaze without apology at others and follow them closely. To keep the group together, we have to watch the leader, not just for the beat, but for subtle indications (sometimes no more than a ghost of a nod) signaling unwritten repeats and holds, and on some songs a swing feel or a rubbery push-pull pulse. Elsewhere, this fixed gaze would be annoying, or even creepy. But when people get up to lead, they expect, and even need, everyone's attention.

So, we look—and sometimes the person in the center has attractions beyond their moving arm. If I'm in the front row, I might be only six or eight feet from the leader. There are few Sacred Harp singers who qualify as eye candy, but some people are very appealing to observe closely, and a few—usually those full of life—are even sexy.

Pretty trebles sit across from handsome basses and it's not surprising that their minds might stray down impure paths. I often face a wall of wailing altos, all female, most unremarkable, but on occasion young and highly distracting.

Driving home from an all-day, Eileen said, "At the break, I noticed everybody got up and started moving around, but you just stood there. And Laura, who'd been sitting with me during that session, said, jokingly, 'Your husband is having impure thoughts.' After considering for a second, I said, 'He can think what he wants as long as the action comes to me.'" Laura thought about it a moment, then gave Eileen a big smile.

"Sometimes a cute guy gets up to lead," Eileen continued. "Often, they turn around 360 degrees in order to enjoy the full sound. And so, I get a perfect view of him from behind. It's a nice shape and it's part of my enjoyment of the person and the whole singing experience."

Many couples wouldn't be so honest or open on this question, but we're long past such primness. "There's an exchange when a person is leading. They're requesting a particular song, often it's one of their favorites, and the group cooperates and gives them what they ask for." We agree that it's foolish to try separating life energy from sexual energy. It's all part of the organic whole: sound, bodies, friendship, food, family, grief, and endless pleasures. "The group gives the leader a gift, and when they sit down, the group gives the next person a gift, until everyone who asks, receives."

There are couples not exactly divided by Sacred Harp but infused with a certain sadness. Most spouses who don't share the obsession have a bemused tolerance. But there are some who can't stand being in the same room as fifty, seventy-five, a hundred shape note devotees in full cry. "How," it seems their pained facial expressions say, "can you love that crude yelling and love me too?" They drop off a covered dish, make a few greetings, and flee. There's sorrow, like a pint of corn liquor poured into a five-gallon punch bowl, that tinctures these marriages. I've never heard of Sacred Harp literally tearing a marriage apart; however, I'm sure that those of us with hard-singing partners in life have an extra bond holding us together. It's sometimes said that all marriages that survive have a third element: children of course, an important job sometimes, a cause that both partners embrace, religion or high ideals. Singing did not save my marriage from the scrap heap (I attribute that to a lot of very serious psychotherapy), but it certainly gave us both a center we could come back to when the going got rough.

INTOXICANTS

Before I had my first serious slug of whiskey (at age forty) and dove headfirst into the deep river of shape note music, I held most country music in contempt. It seemed pitiful, endless whining about drunkenness and adultery. Learning the power of alcohol changed how I saw a man like Hank Williams. He was a slave to the bottle. It was that simple. There was no whiskey he could resist. Some photos of him, near the end of his twenty-nine years on earth, show a haggard, scrawny wretch. One of the most famous, with Hank shirtless and hungover, has iconic status now among a certain slice of his fan base. There's even a new version that makes the half-naked Hank into Saint Sebastian: shot full of arrows. Before any famous rock stars had killed themselves with speed, coke, downers, or heroin, Hank was riding the hell-bound train, and making no excuses.

Yet all the way to the end, he was singing old tymie hymns and gospel songs. One of his best-selling albums (compiled after his death) plays entirely to this. The cover of *I Saw the Light* shows Hank wearing a natty scarf and hat, and a pinched and pious expression. Behind him is a stylized image of a so-called little country church. All the songs are overtly Christian and there's not a whiff of irony in the lot.

Despite all the booze and drugs and desperation, it's "I Saw the Light" that will be forever associated with Hank's life, death, and putative redemption. The song is simple: the three basic chords, rhyming "night" and "sight" and "light." It's built on a pair of well-worn comparisons. Hank tells us that he's like a blind man who wants his vision back and Jesus is like a strange healer-man who comes to him in the darkness of night. The light breaks and he praises the Lord. Simple and direct.

So, is this just straight-up hypocrisy? A drunk and a drug addict, trapped in a hellish marriage, telling the world how good it feels to be saved by Jesus. Sincerity, I've heard it said of country music, is everything. And once you've learned to fake that, you're all set.

On one of our sojourns to Alabama, Eileen and I went all the way to Montgomery, just so that I could enter the sacred precincts of the Hank Williams Museum. Eileen decided to sit that one out. I paid my modest fee and entered alone, breathing the dust of lost days. It was a light day, so I had the place mostly to myself. On display were some of his glitzy cowboy suits, concert posters, and a huge 78 rpm record (a predecessor of 33 rpm long-players.) Best though, and by far most affecting, was the 1952 powder blue Cadillac in perfect condition. This was the death car. I edged in close when no one was looking and stroked my fingertips across the cool blue fender. I gazed into the back seat and pictured Hank going cold there as he headed north.

He set off from Montgomery on December 30, 1952. After taking a shot of morphine to ease his chronic back pain, he began his death drive with Charles Carr (a college boy on Christmas break) at the wheel of his Cadillac. Hank also took chloral hydrate—a bitter white crystalline drug used as a hypnotic and sedative (and in knockout drops).

After the plane he was supposed to take from Knoxville to Canton, Ohio, had to turn back because of fog, Hank and his driver checked into the Andrew Johnson Hotel, where Hank drank Falstaff beer, gave himself two more shots of morphine and one of vitamin B-12.

In the early morning hours of January 1, somewhere in West Virginia between Mt. Hope and Oak Hill, Carr noticed that the blanket had slid off of Hank. He reached back and found Hank's hand was cold and stiff.

The Cadillac was kept in a bay at the Pure Oil gas station in Oak Hill. An autopsy was performed in a mortuary across from the hospital. Cause of his demise: heart failure. In other words, Hank was killed by death.

As far as we know, though Hank grew up in Alabama, he never sang from *The Sacred Harp*. But his live performances and radio shows often included what he called "good old gospel hymns." Sentimental and mawkish, these were big favorites with his lowbrow audience. After his death, the recordings were repackaged and sold by the truckload to listeners who longed for an upright and pure—a sanctified—Hank. But in fact, these tunes were far more modern than *The Sacred Harp,* some of them only a few years old when Hank laid them down on wax.

"Where the Soul of Man Never Dies"
"The Prodigal Son"
"I'll Have a New Body (I'll Have a New Life)"
"When God Comes to Gather His Jewels"

Lying comatose in the back seat of a Cadillac, flying along a snowy West Virginia highway, full of opiates and alcohol: it's hard for me to reconcile that with Hank's vision of transforming light from above.

The same turbid current of contradiction runs through the depths of Sacred Harp. Six hours of yelling about God, then a social, that is, a big party, often with liquor, more music, sometimes with all-night wildness going on in the tents in back and around campfires. If you put dozens of people together, some of them young and full of pent-up sexual energy, then let loose the constraints and decorum of the actual sing, certain behaviors not approved by the church are bound to occur.

This is of course not unique to Sacred Harp. I have a friend who refers to the high points of his teenage summers as "going to Unitarian sex camp." Southern Baptists get divorced far more often than northern Quakers or neo-pagans. Ernest Tubb's hit song, "Saturday Sinner, Sunday Saint," points straight at the hypocrisy of so many country music lovers. A common sight down south is a cluster of men standing around outside a church, surreptitiously passing around a fruit jar while the women are inside hearing the preacher (who may or may not obey the commandment to abjure adultery) exhort them to purity. A Mennonite bishop of my acquaintance lost almost everything when his sexual indiscretions came to light. It seems more poignant though, when the sinner's fans—his true believers—keep clinging to the illusion of sanctity. Nobody defends the erstwhile bishop's sleazy actions, but to this day there are people who insist that Hank went to heaven pure, not filled to the gills with cheap booze and narcotics.

Are Sacred Harp singers abject drunkards like Hank? I don't know a single one who fits into that category. Too much cannabis—sometimes. Unpleasant and unwanted sexual suggestions—there can be some of that. Crazy—even suicidal—driving? Check. Freak-outs and mental breakdowns? Yes indeed—I've seen that too. Weird ideas and bad social skills? We've got plenty of that. Severe halitosis? Yep.

However, what I've just described is normal, or at least very common, and not unique to Sacred Harp. Give yourself to any social organism and you're sure to suffer the usual parade of human frailty. Churches attract a high percentage of this, because most of them have a built-in All Are Welcome agenda. Sacred Harp likewise has no tests nor trials to endure. Show up, give it your best shot, don't do anything that will require us calling the cops, and you're okay to come back next time.

I've never seen or smelled anyone truly drunk at a northern sing. Once though, with our friend Laura, we drove to rural Wayne County (home of the Mormon holy sites) to lead a singing school, and by the time we arrived, I had a blistering migraine. Laura too suffered from these and gave me some of her pills. On the way back, I told her, "Sacred Harp is great, but Sacred Harp on codeine is really great."

DISEMBODIED SAINTS

In *Ecstatic Religion*, anthropologist I. M. Lewis lays out the basic mechanisms of spirit possession and shamanism. Around the world the same elements can be found at work: loud music with a powerful rhythmic pulse, dance or other forms of bodily engagement, long duration of exposure, close physical proximity, a strong sense of the ancestral presence, and mystical surrender "in which man's whole being seems to fuse in a glorious communion with the divinity." All of these elements are present in Sacred Harp.

I knew from the first day I sang the *fa-so-la's* that a thousand other religious rites have much in common with what I was seeing, hearing, and feeling. I understood that Sacred Harp was just another manifestation of a world-wide dynamic. Was it the "Jay-zuss!" of the Primitive Baptists, the Dionysus of the ancient Greeks, or the Damballah of Voodoo rites? Were these angels, gods, ancestors, or "disembodied saints" (as the most popular song in *The Sacred Harp* calls them) that move among us and use our voices to make such a clamor? I chose, early on, to not differentiate between such beings. Different names, but perhaps the same force. I chose to surrender, at least part of myself part of the time.

In ecstatic practice, there is often reference to upper and lower worlds (such as heaven and hell) with the human world connecting the two. Moving between these worlds is the "master of anomaly and chaos"—the shaman. That word gets much overused these days. Drugging and dancing all night to soulless techno does not transform a person into a shaman. Neither does watching videos or paying to be a psychedelic tourist. I'm not criticizing any of these, but I'm aware that shamanism makes huge demands which very few people understand, let alone accept. "The shaman's initiatory experience is represented as an involuntary surrender to disorder, as he is thrust protesting into the chaos which the ordered and controlling life of society strives so hard to deny, or at least keep at bay. No matter how valiantly he struggles, disorder eventually claims him and marks him with the brand of a transcendental encounter."

I make no claim to the status of shaman, nor will I argue that Sacred Harp is a true shamanic phenomenon. In fact, the shaman is the one element that is missing from even the most ecstatic of big sings. There are no stars, no cult of celebrity. Though there are some remarkable voices and people with genuine connections to tradition, Sacred Harp goes on after even the most well-known and well-regarded singers have died. They may remain with us, raised from their netherworld by their favorite songs. But they're not in the center of the square, leading as they once did.

Still, I recognize the fragile balance of order and disorder. High volume, long duration, the blood of Jesus, human sweat, and heartfelt tears: these can combine to break down social structure. Perhaps the rigid jaws of southern men and hard scowls on the faces of southern women are there to hold in the chaos that might erupt at a sing. All the rules (a.k.a. "tradition") may be maintained in order that no one crosses into forbidden territory.

I sing in the old church with old people six hours in a row. I pour myself body and soul into the roar. I shut down my rational mind and let the power of the voice and breath take over. And I'm wrenched out of my ordinary consciousness. In some real way I have journeyed to another time and place.

I have no literal ancestors in Alabama. None of my people in New York State sang from the shape note books. Still, it seems that there is a kind of lineage, a long-buried emotional memory, which comes to life when I sing the old songs.

Some people joke that you either have the gene or don't. Without it, shape note is at best an annoyance. I've seen looks of revulsion—and even fear—on the faces of people lacking the shape note genetic key. All the way to my chromosomes, I feel the pull. For me, if I come late to a sing and hear it from outside, or down the hall, there's a genuine physical attraction, as though I'm a small boat skidding down rapids toward a waterfall. I rush toward the sound, find a seat close to the middle, look over to the guy next to me to see what page we're on, and join in midstream.

I can easily explain away so-called racial memory and archetypes as soft-headed Jungian fantasy. From the outside, it's easy to brush this off as hyped-up self-induced emotionalism. But there's a whisper of doubt in me—what if my cynicism is just a way to avoid a strange and troubling truth? What if the past and present do truly weave into each other, like the overlapping of four-part harmony?

RAISING POWER

Veltin Chafin, the chairman, says, "You come the furthest, you sit up front." At Sardis Church the front bench is mostly old men, serious, if not somber. But this isn't just some Alabama Old Boys Club. There's a relaxed inclusivity I seldom see in other male-dominated situations. No macho bullshit, no competitive posturing, yet something deeply and truly male. This is patriarchy in the best sense: good men who know what they're doing and who do it for a good reason.

The oldest of them have been singing Sacred Harp since the Great Depression. Maybe for some of them it's just ingrained family habit, no deeper than always buying John Deere tractors. But family lineages (three or four generations at some singings) also give purpose and a real sense of connection to the past.

At Sardis, the memorial aspect is overt. This annual gathering honors the Sanders family, who'd worshiped here for decades. There's even the sense that people will literally rejoin their ancestors and "strike the heavenly lyre." While some may smirk at this, others seem to really feel it.

I own a Methodist hymnal from the turn of the last century. Between its covers are some of the old tunes that appear in *The Sacred Harp:* "Pleyel's", "St. Thomas", "Ortonville", "Coronation", "Federal Street", "Cleansing Fountain", "Sessions", "Boylston", "Laban", "Lenox", "Mear", and "Amsterdam". My mother's parents sang these tunes. But I have no fantasy that Hamilton and Ethel ever belted these like folks on Sand Mountain do. I'm sure the versions here in the North were sedate, perhaps even boring. Still, when I went to church with my grandparents, I heard these tunes.

The people at Sardis are in the moment, immersed and unquestioning. But I slip in and out, like a ghost unsure which world is really mine. One moment, I'm sucked into the sound, the sheer physicality of the singing. Then I pull back and observe, reflect, and sometimes twist my experience into knots of irony.

A perfect example of this was my celebration of Louie Louie's fiftieth birthday. Exactly one-half century before, the great and mighty "Louie Louie" was recorded. The Kingsmen went into the studio in Portland, Oregon, and did only one take of the greatest occult song in the history of rock and roll. Thus "Louie Louie" entered the world. Not Richard Berry's original fake calypso version, not the one cut by the Raiders, the Sonics, the Wailers, or the hundreds of other bands who've attempted to capture the essence. There is only one true primal Louie Louie.

Exactly fifty years later, to celebrate, I led an all-day shape note singing on the other side of the continent. Forty adepts came from hundreds of miles away to raise their voices with me. From Toronto, Buffalo, central Pennsyltucky, Erie, Albany, Utica, Ithaca, they came to a little Mennonite church to eat pig and yell about the gods. And to conjure with me the ghost of Louie Louie.

Modern day witches talk about "raising power." Catholics feel true reverence in the presence of the consecrated host. Muslim pilgrims experience transforming power as they near the Kaaba. Snake handling Christians feel a holy anointing which protects them from deadly venom.

All of these are spiritual cousins of Sacred Harp. As a singing heats up, there's foot stomping, rocking in the seats, and rhythmic head-bobbing. Little kids dance. Old people seem animated by the spirit of earlier times. The power usually peaks after our lunch break. Full of caffeine and sugar, somewhat rested, people return to the square eager to amp up the speed and volume.

The average human body emits heat that's equal to a 100-watt light bulb. So, on a primal level the singing can be rated in watts. A hundred people packed into a room generate 10,000 watts of body heat. Breath is internal moisture—body steam. Oxygen rushes in and carbon dioxide pours out. Sweat and tears evaporate. The moving molecules of air have a pressure, a billion tiny hammers, like Watt's original steam engine capturing the release of boiling water. Energy rises with the day—caffeine, sugar and pork fueling the engine.

For a physicist, watts = volts (pressure) × amps (quantity). To rate the power of a Sacred Harp sing, you could multiply the pressure (that is: the volume and intensity of the voices) times the quantity (that is: number of songs in a row) times the number of singers.

In truth I never really do the math. But I felt the motive power as I stood in the center of the square leading, secretly celebrating, a half century of Louie Louie.

The song still lurks in the airwaves, cryptic and incoherent. The lyrics are a black Los Angeles version of Jamaican patois ("me see me love") but were rumored to be obscene, childish, drug-related, even Communist propaganda. The FBI spent two and a half years investigating. Playing the song hundreds of times at 16, 33, 45 and 78 rpm, they finally admitted defeat, unable to decipher the mysterious lyrics.

The Kingsmen version—which sold eight million copies—is notable mostly for its ragged incompetence. Especially remarkable is the drumming by soon-to-be-King of the Kingsmen, Lynn Eastman. A more cloddish banging on a Top 40 hit is impossible to find. The guitar solo and keyboard riffing might've passed muster in somebody's garage, but few other places. The 1-4-5 chords are the same as in thousands of other songs. And Jack Ely's vocal—a wild adolescent yawp—is hardly the stuff of genius.

Energy and sheer abandon more than make up for what this cut lacks. Other bands are faster, louder, harder, sexier, and far more skilled. Ten thousand singers are better than Jack Ely. And anyone—or anything with opposable thumbs—can play drums better than Lynn Eastman. Still, the Kingmen's "Louie Louie" is the One—the Maximum Louie from Dimension X. It is the wizard's brew and witch's broom that swept eight million teenagers into an ecstatic trance.

How many other singers understood my secret delight in this Sacred Harp birthday gathering? None. I'd highjacked the singing for my own private purpose and no one else knew or cared. But that didn't matter. Because, as the Rastafarian wise man says, "He who feels it knows it."

I felt—I knew—the arcane power ringing off four plain white walls. Drunk on the noise, adepts came to the middle and called out their tunes.

> "World Unknown"
> "My Life and Breath"
> "Immensity"
> "Sweet Affliction"
> "David's Lamentation"

If I'd grown up in Alabama, then I might experience the singing without uncertainty or ironic distance. I'd just do it and feel it. But I dwell in an interzone. I can let go for a while and really feel it: the voices of the dead wailing through my body. Then I'm back here at this table, alone in silence. I think and dissect, remember and write, disconnected from my body.

A STRANGER HERE BELOW

I ride a Pennsyltucky time machine: the all-day singing at an eighteenth century meetinghouse. No lights, no electricity, no screens on the windows, no running water or toilets, and horsehair cushions on the creaking benches.

The building itself was moved decades back, when a thousand acre reservoir was created, the entire structure picked up, along with dozens of graves, and moved to higher ground. Now, its original place is fathoms down, buried in water.

Here, in this meetinghouse saved from drowning and oblivion, I celebrate my birthday with six hours of four-part wailing.

After the singing, dozens of us go to Zane's farm, far out in the late summer backlands, past acres of corn. "Go left at the old mushroom sheds and then left again at the Red Boar."

There's music everywhere at Zane's: fiddles, banjos, an out-of-tune piano, singing indoors and out. There are people camping in the fields and by the lily pond, plenty of fresh-killed meat, and young people "romping," as Zane told me with a gap-toothed leer and a rheumy wink. He also told me—downing another beer—about the shadow side of nineteenth-century revivals. "After hours of preaching and praying and carrying-on, folks got pretty frisky. They used to say that more souls were made than saved."

The previous tenants on Zane's farm were a family of Nicaraguan refugees, with eight kids and no hot water. There have been changes since then, opening some boarded-up windows and doors, but the house still has the feel of a haphazard maze.

The main stairway splits at the second floor, leading to dim, musty rooms. In one of the bedchambers, a tree has grown in from outside, eager branches groping their way in between gaps in two window frames, the exterior world penetrating the interior spaces.

On the first floor, one room is heaped with arcane junk, and from the bare ceiling joists hang a dozen old marching band instruments like tarnished silver fruit: cornets, miniature euphoniums, and field horns. The cases of old fiddles and guitars are stacked against one wall, like half-size coffins.

Someone asks how many cats he has, and Zane says, "Maybe a dozen, or fifteen." Dogs lay like mats of fur.

Zane carves the roast turkey. The handles on his big knife and fork are made of deer antler, twisted and stained with old animal juices. He serves the last of the corn from his garden. "The kernels are big, but I think they're still sweet," he says.

Out back is the summer kitchen. The fireplace there is huge, with a massive oak beam for a mantelpiece. The stored remains of a hundred-year-old cookery are heaped in the little building: the wooden dasher from a butter churn, tin plates and pans, wrought iron fire tongs.

There's an underground vault not far from the main house, used in the nineteenth century for storing wine and meat. This year, I gather up a small procession and descend with them into the dank, lightless vault.

Not quite drunk, but full of wild spirits, we go down the steps and push open the door. Inside, a half dozen of us sing, testing the acoustics, testing ourselves against the subterranean gloom, making echoes, rattling the dank stone walls. It's only eleven steps down to the vault, but there, with the door shut behind us (like a prison cell, a secret hiding place, a mausoleum) we make our rough harmonies ring.

There's a wrecked wooden barrel in the vault and I kick it in time with the singing, making a bass drum thump for the song called **"Plenary"** (which means complete and fully attended.) The words are by Watts; the melody is the northland tune used by Burns for "Auld Lang Syne," which means old long ago.

> Hark! from the tomb a doleful sound,
> Mine ears, attend the cry,
> Ye living men, come view the ground
> Where you must shortly lie.
>
> "Princes this clay must be your bed,
> In spite of all your tow'rs.
> The tall, the wise, the rev'rend head,
> Must lie as low as ours."
>
> Great God! Is this our certain doom?

> And are we still secure?
> Still walking downward to the tomb,
> And yet prepared no more!

Then we go upward, and emerge, blinking and woozy, into the heavy late summer light. Around the bank of the pond in back are the biggest lily pads I've ever seen, three feet across floating in the scum-choked water. And scattered among them are massive bulbous flowers, like ancient lotus blooms.

In one of the gardens, Eileen finds a praying mantis. I haven't seen one of them since childhood. It's brown and green and long as my forefinger. Like everything at the farm, it too seems something escaped from a dream.

I lean in close to get a better look at the mantis as she chews leisurely at a morsel—probably the brain of Mr. Mantis—in her upraised front legs. I get nearer and the bug turns her head to look at me, as though I were the strange specimen and not she. Her head shifts on her neck. She seems so human, with her eyes facing me in challenge, as if to say, "What do you want?"

I back away, feeling a little tremor of dread.

Just as the sun is bleeding out its last watery crimson, the remaining guests gather at the big dining room table to sing. Eileen and I make a little space of elbow room, pushing back a stack of sheet music and a frayed fiddle bow. The main door is propped open for a bit of damp breeze. No screens, so moths and beetles batter around the lights in the ceiling fixture, three ordinary incandescents and one sickly-red bulb.

There are nine of us, enough for a full sound on all

four parts. The first tune we do—and my favorite that night—is an obscure old one called **"Conflict."** We use a new shaped note arrangement, melding harmonies from two different books. It's a weird, plaintive, deeply sad piece and our uncertain voices add to the shifting major/minor melancholy sound.

> I am a stranger here below.
> And what I am is hard to know.
> Like one alone, I seem to be.
> Oh, is there anyone like me?

All of us lean into the tune, coaxing a ghost voice out of its dreamy coffin earth. We sing for two hours, but that one tune follows me home in my mind's ear. Like a voice from two hundred years gone, but somehow issuing from my own mouth.

Exhausted and drunk on the heat, we say goodbye and wander up the long dark gravel driveway. The whir of the night insects is loud and insistent, maybe echoing the raw singing from inside.

As my eyes get used to the starless dark, I can see the swell and fall of farmland acres. A barn maybe a mile away stands solid as a tombstone. Somewhere far off a sprinkler hisses and whooshes like a mechanical version of the peepers. And from even farther away comes the cry of some creature I can't identify. Bird, beast, spirit? It's hooty and insistent like an owl but has some of the eerie sadness of a horse's whinny.

UTOPIAN TRACE

I'd gotten a glimpse, a taste, an echo, a whiff, of the Old Weird America. I like that phrase, which Greil Marcus coined, taking off from Kenneth Rexroth's "old free America." But free for whom, I wondered. Slaves, Indians, women, children, followers of strange faiths? Marcus changed it to the Old *Weird* America and that rang for me with a deeper truth.

He used the term to describe the world out of which so much haunted and haunting music was born. In particular, Marcus wrote at length about the *Anthology of American Folk Music*, a six-record box set released in 1952. But all the recordings it contained were made between 1927 and 1933: murder ballads, hymns, raw blues, sermons, nonsense songs going back hundreds of years to Britain, fiddle tunes, Cajun one steps and jug band stomps. It even contains two songs about presidential assassins: Guiteau (the noose), and Czolgosz (the electric chair).

The *Anthology* is a deep mine shaft into the heart of the Old Weird America. Its influence on the folk revival of the '50s and '60s was enormous. It's safe to say that without it we might never have heard of Dylan and the Band and all their followers. Without it, few Deep North folkies would've gone south to find what the southerners never completely gave up, and I might never have heard of Sacred Harp.

The entire collection, eighty-four lost and found recordings, is a kind of occult amulet. The original box set came with bizarre notes (by Harry Smith, the compiler), cryptic clipart illustrations, and quotes from Robert Fludd, a seventeenth-century pantheistic alchemist. The version I stumbled on in the early '70s was on 3 LP records, with a cover showing an abject, penniless depression-era farmer. Listening to such bizarreries as "I Wish I Was a Mole in the Ground" and "The Coo Coo Bird," I felt (even if I didn't understand) the sheer powerful otherness of these recordings.

There are only two Sacred Harp cuts on the Anthology, and they made little impression on me. As a young man I was searching for dark-heart blues, damnation country, forays into the graveyard. Decades later, the banjos and fiddles, the quavering panpipes and wheezing mouth organs still sound wonderful. But it's the human voice that reigns over them all. Some of the singers were still alive when the Anthology first came out, but young listeners assumed they were long gone into the world of the dead. To connect, to grab a tenuous hold on this almost-lost world, some singers memorized every song on the set. It's said that when neo-folkie performers started in on "Omi Wise" or "See That My Grave Is Kept Clean," everybody in the little coffee houses would stand and sing along.

Some have called this allure *the utopian trace*—a tiny flicker of what once was. But the Old Weird America was hardly a utopia. Brutal inequality, genocide, industrial rape of the earth, mad capitalist greed: the list is long and horrible to contemplate. Still, if this trace element isn't just sentimental bullshit, then what do I truly experience?

I'd seen and heard—and been inside—the hundred-strong hollow square. I'd drunk the corn liquor and eaten the biscuits soaked in pig grease. I'd sucked in the smell of churches made—ceiling, walls, and floor—of raw timber seasoned for a hundred, two hundred, years. But still, I wondered sometimes: was I just a postmodern tourist?

If all this oldness, weirdness, and Americana was just a quaint trace of a never-never past, then I was living in self-delusion. If it's no better than collectible antiques for rich childless couples' summer homes; if it's just books to fetishize, riffling the pages and huffing the dusty fumes; if it's the equivalent of Amish kitsch or so-called Alabama heritage, if it's no more significant than Civil War re-enactors wearing authentic wool underwear—then we were all fakers and fools.

THE WHISKEY SING

Like the Farmer's Museum in Cooperstown (where I'd seen the Cardiff Giant and sung temperance songs in an eighteenth-century tavern), like the Old Alabama Town in Montgomery (where we'd gone after the Hank Williams Museum), the Genesee Country Village is both fake and genuine. The buildings are authentic, carefully transported from all across New York State, lovingly restored to their archaic charm and open to the public. But the village—68 buildings on 600 acres—was artificially assembled. Before John Wehle (who made his fortune on Genesee Beer) bought the grounds and began saving old buildings, the village had been farmland that had reverted to a wild state.

Over the years, our local group was invited to sing at the Village, the largest of its kind in the state. The last time was by far the best. Singers came from far around, drawn by the allure of Sacred Harp in a genuine nineteenth century building. With most of the windows sealed shut, it was hot, close, and wonderfully loud. Even the smell of the hard wooden benches and raw plank floor worked to conjure a different time and place, an escape from the soulless ugliness of modern life.

Eileen wasn't able to go that day. We'd been joking that this would be our wedding anniversary sing but she'd gotten food poisoning the day before and couldn't get out of bed.

Deeply disappointed that I was heading off alone on our anniversary, I arrived at the sing drunk. The drive was about an hour, and on the way, I stopped at a little liquor store to buy three shooters of whiskey. Parking at the Village, I knocked all three shots back. Lugging a box full of loaner books far across the great meadow in full sunshine further addled my brain.

Compared to some championship drunks, I was barely under the influence. Yet I felt it: a sloppiness, a looseness, a I-don't-give-a damn attitude. Without Eileen's treble voice in the mix, the event seemed off-kilter. Out of the hundreds of sings I'd been to, she had only been missing two or three times. Her place was at my right, not an anchor, but a wing-like lateen sail, catching the gospel breeze and helping to pull us through the waves.

Did others know how inebriated I was? If so, no one let on. We were packed in tightly, so the fumes must've wafted into the hollow square. Years back I'd learned that alcohol, even one beer, dries out the vocal cords and weakens the voice. Still, I was relentless that day. I pitched both sessions and did a good job of it. I sat on the front bench and gave it my all.

As I expected, without hearing Eileen's clear unaffected treble voice on my right, the group just wasn't the same. There were other good singers on her part, but my entire foray into Sacred Harp had been with Eileen literally in my corner, our voices meeting at a ninety-degree angle.

Guests to the Village came and went. Some wormed their way past the knots of people at both doors and stood for a while admiring our enthusiasm, if not the beauty of the sound. A few took pictures, but we weren't in cutesy period costumes. Some held up their devices to record our din. What they caught, I'm sure, captured barely a trace of the real sound.

We took a break about halfway through the sing and I went, in a daze, to wander the Village. My favorite building there is an octagon house, transported from the town of Friendship about fifty miles away. I'd been fascinated by the octagon style since first encountering it in college. Barns, houses, even outhouses: thanks to the evangelical efforts of Orson Fowler (also a leader in the phrenology craze): our region has plenty of fine examples of this quasi-occult nineteenth century fad.

Back at the little schoolhouse, I was feeling less elated than when I'd arrived. Yet, until the last song, I was front and center, leading the group, blasting at the sunshine, conjuring the shadows.

We finished that day with "Panting for Heaven."

> I'm fettered and chained up in clay.
> I struggle and pant to be free.
> I long to be soaring away
> My God and my Savior to see.

ECSTASY

At Antioch, late in the afternoon, as the passion of the singing reached its peak, an old woman stood up at the back of the church and began wailing and gibbering, waving her hands and flailing her tongue. She had gobs of hot-pink makeup on her wizened cheeks, and her coppery hair stuck out like wire sprung from a blown transformer. I couldn't understand a word she said, and the two men in charge of the singing froze with embarrassment. She went on and on in her crazed ululating monologue, like she'd lost everything in the world.

When she paused, the chairman jumped in and called another song. "Number 106!" Maybe it was a coincidence, or maybe it's traditional practice at Antioch: the song called "Ecstasy" was next. The chairman let loose his *fa-la-so* pitches to give us the key, and the old lady was buried back in the roaring sound.

Lonnie Louie told me afterward that they never let it slide all the way into an old-style meeting where order breaks down into a raw outpouring of religious squalling. "At a big sing, they don't want anybody getting too Jesus-happy," as Lonnie Louie put it. "People come to sing, not to hear testifying." To keep the wildness in check, all the passion goes straight into the music. They don't let the boundaries collapse when their young people are present. "Too much, too soon. Not a good idea." The structures remain steady, or if they slip a little, they are quickly put back in place.

"You got to have enough folks all together for the spirit to come down. Least that's what my brother-in-law says." In other words, it may be that the wild release only takes place in an atmosphere of true oneness. Certainly, at times the singing seems to forge itself into a seething organic whole: a hundred voices issuing from one swarm-like being. Without unanimity, family, and generations of history, the breaking loose of the spirit might be impossible.

North or south, I never once heard in church anybody preach or teach on Nietzsche. But maybe he understood the heart of religious ecstasy better than any theologian. "The bond between one person and another is re-forged by the spell of Dionysus. Each person finds himself not only united and blended with another, but is in fact truly fused, as though the veil of illusion had been torn apart and was fluttering now in shreds before the primordial mystery of unity."

Long before Jesus, there came Dionysus. And though most Christians will say there's no connection between the two gods-in-human-form, their origins, lives, powers, and deaths are rife with mythic parallels.

The Lord chose Mary to bear his son and his birth was announced by a sky-full of brilliant angels, singing, of course. Dionysus was the son of Zeus and a mortal. He was born in a lightning blast, killing the mother. Dionysus was the god of mad revelation, revelry, and wine. Jesus said, "I am the vine" and the sacramental wine is his blood. The first miracle Jesus did was turning water into wine. In Matthew 11 it's said that "the Son of Man came eating and drinking, and everyone said 'Behold a man gluttonous and a wino, a friend of barkeeps and sinners.'"

To watch, to hear, or much better, to stand in the middle of a big sing, it's clear that the god who people are yelling about isn't the milquetoast savior of mainstream Christianity. Sacred Harp is both thoroughly Christian and profoundly pagan, existing both inside and outside the realm of monotheistic religion.

"It's the only place," Eileen has pointed out more than once, "where I've experienced believers and nonbelievers singing hymns together—for the sheer joy of it. It's not a worship setting, but for some people it is genuinely worshipful. There are people who are communing with God, or the Holy Spirit, or whatever you want to call it. And yet when it feels like the group is lifting off the ground, everybody feels it, no matter what they believe. I remember a pastor saying years ago that people go to church for three reasons: community, meaning, and transcendence. When you sing Sacred Harp, you get transcendence."

How much of a stretch, I'm asking myself now, is it to see the Dionysus of ancient Greece and the Jesus of Sand Mountain as being pretty much the same god?

JESUS IS MY GIRLFRIEND

> While on His breast I lean my head,
> And breathe my life out sweetly there.

I might subtly sneer and roll my eyes, singing that one. Still, there's something in these words that haunts me. What makes for better poetic kitsch than a happy homo-affectional death?

> I will rise—and go to Jesus.
> He'll embrace me in His arms.
> In the arms of my dear Savior,
> O there are ten thousand charms.

These eighteenth-century words have been set to dozens of melodies: the most famous Jesus-is-My-Girlfriend lyrics ever penned. Just in *The Sacred Harp*, there are four different versions. They also make up the chorus of the much beloved and often sung, "Ten Thousand Charms," which was introduced in 1996. People—including me—are writing new tunes now. Most—including most of mine—fall by the wayside, xeroxes handed out at sings and left behind when people take off for the day.

I have friends who own Sacred Harp books all the way back to the beginning, and before: the legendary 1810 *Wyeth's Repository*, the first book to use the patented four shape system. I own a 1971 and a 1966 revision of *The Sacred Harp*. Even these two fairly recent editions contain now-vanished vestigial remains from the nineteenth century: "The Teacher's Farewell," "The Red Sea Anthem," "The Spiritual Sailor" and the mystery-packed "Masonic Ode."

The last revision of *The Sacred Harp* came out in 1991, when a handful of new tunes were added and a few dozen older shape note tunes from other books were added. The updating process is painful. If someone suggests removing an old tune with hoary lineage, there's sure to be someone who squawks that "my daddy loved this one so much." Or elders get all teary and declare, "If you take this one out, it means you don't care a damn about the tradition."

It's all but impossible to create a tune that's genuinely new and at the same time fits within the tradition. With unspoken rules and expectations, there's almost nowhere to go after the great tunes were created. So, like modern versions of rockabilly, bebop, the sonnet, Dixieland, and the classical symphony, new shape note tunes usually feel derivative or merely forgettable.

"Ten Thousand Charms," the first shape note tune that Hal Kunkel wrote, manages the nearly miraculous feat of feeling old and new at the same time. Nearly thirty years after the tune's creation, it continues to get singers charged up and sparking with excitement. A group will still on occasion stand spontaneously on the line "I will rise and go to Jesus." Hal's compositional tactics are subtle—just the right variations to make the song both distinctive and traditional.

Though some hard-nosed Christians want the words of the verse to fit into standard theology, Hal's setting has more to do with fiery glossolalia than salvific blood.

> Teach me some melodious sonnet,
> Sung by flaming tongues above.

Yes indeed—flaming tongues, as at the first Pentecost at the first Antioch.

I will rise. Yes—when the elements come perfectly together, it feels as though we're rising, not quite levitating, but definitely caught in an upward-rushing current.

The inspiration for the melody came from Office Depot, not a heavenly summit. Years later, Hal told me, "I was shopping for stationary because I was in the process of working on another song and I needed graph paper to work out the harmonies." In the store, he heard four notes played on the PA system: E E B G#. This was just a bland corporate announcement ditty, barely a melody. "But I'm not discounting a spiritual hand in some of it, at least it was feeling that way to me as the composition progressed." Hal took the fragment and made it into one or the most popular shape note tunes that's not in *The Sacred Harp*. I loved it the first time I heard it, and at the first big sing where I got up my courage to lead, that's the tune I called.

At the time, I was swept up in the rhythmic pull of the tune, the anticipation of the downbeat and the perfect lead-in to the chorus. It wasn't until later I wondered about the rich murky eros in the lyrics. What exactly, I wondered, are these ten thousand charms that Jesus has to offer?

To my right, on the wall, as I write these words, is the funeral home fan I snuck out of a sing in Alabama. Gazing at my stolen souvenir, I end up with more questions than answers. It shows a beautiful Jesus, painted in the style of a 1950s Sunday School handout. He's all in white, standing at a wooden door, with his pale fist ready to tap-tap-tap. The doorway is surrounded by what appear to be blooming thistles. The meaning of this Scottish symbol—if any—is lost on me. The caption at the bottom reads "Rev. 3:20. Behold I stand at the door and knock."

This Jesus is about as white as he could be. His eyes are green, his hair is a pretty shade of auburn, his cheeks are rosy, and I'm positive he got into the lipstick before posing for this painting.

He's not so much effeminate as anti-masculine. Even with the full red beard and the jutting jaw, he seems devoid of sexual identity. With all that drapey white cloth, all that mysterious light glowing around him, it's hard to see him as the divine male offspring. Maybe the strange nephew with pouty lips—but not the son of God. Some preteen girls might think him sufficiently nonthreatening to be cute. I find him a bit distressing to contemplate. But it's not the lipstick and gorgeous hair. For me, it's hard to trust a guy who seems to have a couple 100-watt bulbs hidden inside his robe.

FIRST IN HEAVEN

What's printed on the page tells the story of layered history. What individuals do to their *Sacred Harps* tells a more personal story. Circles, checkmarks, stars, and plusses—these make up informal rating systems. Some guys use complex arrays of bookmarks, making their books look like multi-colored birds or exotic tropical fish. The edges of many copies of *The Sacred Harp* are decorated: Scottish tartans, Irish scrollwork, teen-hipster skulls, childish scrawl. Some people craft handsome cloth covers with pockets. Others mangle their books and toss them around like trash. Mine ended up bandaged with carpenter's glue and old denim.

I found out that someone had beavered through decades of minute books and crunched the numbers to give a statistical analysis of the popularity of each song. I transcribed these numbers (in pencil, so that they could be updated) page by page, and sometimes announced, "that's the 533rd least popular song in the book. And now we know why." Clearly there are songs that will be expunged when the new edition is finally published.

And others are so well beloved that there will be a revolution in the square if they are ever replaced.

Some singers who'd been at it for decades grew tired of the same songs, though it was clear that certain of them are the hooks that bring new people in. The big budget Hollywood film *Cold Mountain* served as an opener of the way for many new singers. Trying to capture a certain downhome authenticity, the filmmakers used two songs, not just on the soundtrack but on screen too. They recorded real Alabama singers. However, the people we see on screen are extras from Romania (where much of the film was shot) who had to be coached to hold their faces and mouths in the rigid Deep South manner as they lip-synched to the Sand Mountain sound. After the movie came out, there was a significant spike in popularity for the two songs used: "I'm Going Home" and "Idumea."

Both of these tunes are great, and few of us have grown tired of them. Others got used up, done to death, sing after sing. Some have been so overdone that certain groups have put a moratorium on their use.

I had what I foolishly admitted was my "toilet list"—about ten songs that I used for bodily relief. Once people figured out that these were the songs I'd grown tired of (or never liked) and used to make a quick exit, it became a running joke. A tune would get called, I'd get up, and there would be a flicker of knowing smiles. I'd written this list on the inside back cover of my book, but eventually erased it.

"Jacob's Vision" was on my list, but not because it was a bad song. In fact, I knew it before I came to Sacred

Harp and liked it quite a bit. However, in the local group, month after month, one of our basses called it every single time, and insisted that we do all three verses and repeat on the chorus.

I liked Hugh. He was smart, he came almost every time, and he helped hold the bass section together. But his attachment to "Jacob's Vision" became wearisome. I didn't complain though. It's an unwritten (though not unspoken) law that everybody gets to pick whatever they like and lead it at whatever tempo they want. Hugh was there in his black leather vest the first time I showed up. Early on, he knew the tradition better than I, and I showed him the respect he was due.

Still, when the choice came around to him, I'd sink a little in my chair, sigh perhaps too audibly, and get myself ready for another go at the ladder that reaches to the "regions of light" and the "mansions of bliss."

Then we heard that Hugh had cancer and we didn't see him in the square anymore. Nearing the end, most of us from the local group went to the hospital to visit him. He couldn't sing anymore; barely a whisper came from his lips. But he was awake and aware enough to request songs. We did what he wanted, surrounding his bed. He mouthed the words and moved his arm, as if leading the group. On the way out, a college age girl was who new to the tradition asked, "Is he going to make it?" She looked stricken and shaky. Perhaps this was the first time she'd been with someone approaching the end.

I said, "No. I don't think so."

We hadn't come to cheer him up, though I did see genuine joy in Hugh's eyes. We'd come to help him die.

> Let music charm me last on earth,
> And greet me first in heav'n.

I'd seen those words stitched on a sampler, hanging on the wall somewhere in Pennsyltucky. They're from a song that doesn't get done very often in the north.

People came from over a hundred miles away to sing at Hugh's funeral. He was a Unitarian, so there was no mention of the afterlife or a savior that day, except in our songs.

MR. JOHNNY

The Lee family flew up from Hoboken, Georgia to be special guests at the annual New York State Convention. With a distinctive style, and a certain level of celebrity among Sacred Harp singers, the Lees were a big draw. It's a long way from the Okefenokee Swamp to the foothills of the Adirondack Mountains, but the Lee family made the trek and shared with us a taste of their ways.

Tollie was in his mid-sixties, extroverted, passionate, loud, and, at times, literally in my face. At the end of a long prayer on Sunday, during which he paced round and round, facing various folks, he ended up practically on top of me, fixing me with his spirit-filled gaze. I noticed that the other Lee men would look back at him, nodding as he faced them during the prayer. So that's what I did too. And the result was that as his voice came down off the chanting high, gasping for breath, he was right in front of me and our eyes locked. It seemed like both a challenge and a blessing: the elder singing me out for a final blast of spiritual power.

David Lee is only one year older than I, a tall, husky

guy who led most of the singing school, and for whom tears came early and often. When the convention rose to clap and thank the Lees for venturing up north, David sat with his face in his hands, weeping in gratitude and humility.

But it was John D. Lee, or Mr. Johnny, to whom I found myself most drawn. He was the least prominent of the Georgia men who'd come to our convention, leading none of the singing school and praying with a more calm and inward affect.

Mr. Johnny's posture was erect, though not stiff. My first thought meeting him was of Clay Lewis, who'd been a Marine, and forty years later still stood like one. Mr. Johnny gave the impression of being more dignified, and more formal, than the others southern guests. He wore pants with serious creases, suede saddle shoes, and a knitted vest under his tweed jacket.

He was born only a few years after my father, and it was moving for me to see father and son—David and Mr. Johnny—sitting together in the bass section. In appearance they weren't obviously kin. But there was a comfort, and a bond between them that I envied.

As the weekend proceeded, it became obvious how proud Mr. Johnny was of his son. He looked on while David taught and told stories of his childhood. The whole while, the expression on his face said, "This is my son and I'm very glad."

At the Saturday night social, when the Lee family sang from Lloyd's hymnal (just words, no music) and taught fifty or so New Yorkers the melodies and harmonies, I sat next to Mr. Johnny. He leaned in close to me and turned to the side so that I could hear his voice clearly, trying to teach me the line he was singing. On the other side was another tenor. Neither of us were in Mr. Johnny's range, but he moved his hand in the air to mark the rising and falling of the line and we tried our hardest to follow. When we came to the end of a song, Mr. Johnny would smile and nod his approval.

When we left the singing that night, I thought—very clearly and unapologetically—"I want him to be my father." There was a dignity to him, a forthright quality, that I admired. He'd been married for over fifty years and talked about his wife as "the most wonderful girl in the world." Though rather formal at first, he showed a good sense of humor, laughing at his son's stories of how strict he'd been. "Me and Daddy didn't do too much negotiating in those days."

On Sunday afternoon, we left for home, and I was gripped by a panic attack: chest pains, shortness of breath, dizziness. And what came rushing back to me was a memory of the last time I'd seen Clay Lewis, and the panic I'd felt when we'd parted.

We had been in D.C. for a singing convention. I was driving around the beltway, heading back to our hotel after a wonderful three-hour talk, full of affirmation, assurance, and most important, approval. Clay had been speaking to me as an equal, as a teacher and a writer. But he was still in the role of elder, a kind of father to me. As we left him, I was sure I was having a heart attack. I could barely breathe. I kept thinking I should pull over. Eileen had been through this with me before, and tried to be reassuring, saying that everything was going to be all right.

But the separation had been wrenching. Clay had looked old, though was still vigorous. He was talking about limits and slowing down and loss. (He'd been married three times and said he didn't think he'd live to see his youngest daughter grow to adulthood.) And I thought as we drove away that I would never see him again. As it turned out, this was right.

The same feeling swept over me as we left the convention. Though Mr. Johnny invited us to come down to Georgia to visit him, and to sing with the Lees (and the invitation was genuine), I knew that I'd never see him again. The echo I got, of fatherly approval, would not be repeated.

MEMORIAL LESSON #2

On the first night of the Garden State Sacred Harp Convention, the woman in charge asked me to do the memorial lesson the next day. She scares me sometimes, but I like Gina. She's big, powerful, very direct and has the loudest unamplified voice I've ever encountered. I probably would've said yes to another person in the same situation (she was running the convention with very little help), but I took it as a compliment that she trusted I could handle the task with very short notice. I said I'd do it, and what came out, with no notes, no text to lean on, no one to help me, was better than I'd expected.

I started by telling the convention about my father, and the facts about outliving him. I told the gathered singers about crossing the line—51 years, 6 months, 24 days. And I told them how much fear had attended crossing that life boundary.

Next, I described the German songbook I'd recently been given by my father's oldest boyhood friend. It was from him that I discovered the source of the songs I'd heard when I was a little kid. The one sung most frequently in our house was *"Wenn die Soldaten, durch die statt marchiren."*

Joined by a third teenager, they would sing together from this tattered book. It's missing a cover and title page, so the publication date can only be guessed at. How old were these boys when they pushed their voices through such hyper-German volkische songs? Though the Bund flourished in Rochester, it was dead by 1941. And Germany's enemy status was firmly established by the time my father was in high school. Yet the three of them got together and sang these German songs as high school kids. 1942, '43, '44? What teenager facing the draft in 1945 would dare sing such words?

Some of the songs refer directly to boys and young men. *"Burschen Heraus! Lasset es schallen von Haus zu Haus."* (Boys—to the outdoors! Let it ring from house to house.) *"Ich hatt einen Kameraden"* (which was sung at General Erwin Rommel's funeral). This is not strictly Hitler-Jugend stuff. There's no Storm Trooper thuggery here. Still, it's definitely a cousin of such music: outdoorsy, hyper-male, hearty, ripe with gang companionship.

When he was in a good mood (which was not very often) my father sang these loud, Wandervogel-style hiking songs at home. Along with swimming, it was one of the fleeting ways his life-force (joy, strength, humor) came out. I think, if he could've gotten past the intimidating factors in shaped note singing, my father would've liked it very much: loud, raw, unpretentious.

Gina's husband told me at lunch—right after I gave the memorial lesson—that the Wandervogel tradition had had a direct impact on him being at the convention that day. He went through a long, convoluted chain of connections, (starting with the cheap recorders for the wandering volkisch minstrels in Germany) and ended up with him (a Jew from California) interested in American folk hymnody and shaped note music. Now he's learning plattdeutsch so he can speak with the Amish.

After the memorial lesson singing of "Soft Music" (which is "*Du, du liegst mir im Herzen*" filtered through a southern gospel sensibility) I moved on to the so-called sick and shut-in list. I described an old friend who's had AIDS for decades, yet still has a better outlook on life than most people I know. A link to my father (beside my friend's role as a crypto-paternal advocate for me) is his self-description as "looking like a Hitler Youth." It's true. When he was younger, he had Aryan blond hair and Teutonic good looks, just as the pictures of my father show him in his twenties.

Over the years, I've kept my friend up to date with my shaped note adventures. Though a successful Manhattanite with no taste for eating pig and yelling about God, still he's consistently interested in my reports from the field. Strange and noxious foods (e.g. roadkill venison casserole, fried pie) are of particular interest.

Then I moved on to talk about another friend—also a musician—who is being steadily consumed by madness. "There are diseases of the body that afflict us," I said in New Jersey. "But everyone in this room knows someone afflicted by mental illness so awful that it's impossible to tolerate." I didn't use the word "suicide," but people knew what I was talking about. "We can help to bear each other's burdens, but for some there's little we can offer beside our presence."

I closed with a few words about William Cowper, who wrote the lyrics for **"Cleansing Fountain"** and other shape note favorites. "Some modern scholars have assumed that he was what we'd now call bipolar. But there are places in his poetry when it seems that he's not just depressed but already dead. In the song we call '**Cambridge**,' Cowper describes his abysmal state as though he were not even human—unable to even experience suffering. We're going to sing that now for all the people we know who carry this unbearable pain."

> I hear but seem to hear in vain,
> Insensible as steel;
> If aught is felt, 'tis only pain,
> To find I cannot feel.

ARDENT SPIRITS

Kester told me to never drink moonshine unless you know who made it. "They run it through junk car radiators—instead of the old way with copper tubing—all kinds of poison in that. But if you trust the fella who made it, no reason not to enjoy a couple of swigs."

Inspired by Kester's wisdom, and the craftsmanship of his cousins, the corn mash conjurers, I tried my hand at creating homemade whiskey. I sprouted my own barley malt and shopped for the best yeast for such an undertaking. (The guy at Beers of the World was helpful but wanted me to understand that distilling without a license was strictly illegal.) I settled on champagne yeast, which could survive at the highest proof before dying in its own excretion, which is alcohol. With a few gallons of cooked corn meal and a little white sugar, I had a mash that seethed and bubbled in a most pleasing manner. I have a friend whose taste in beer runs toward what he calls "liquid bread." What fermented in my kitchen was exactly that. I let it sit, unmolested, for four days, until the head was a bubbling, amber-brown foam, then began the arcane process of extracting the spiritous essence.

Distillation is the earliest act of scientific magic: liquifying, lifting and condensing the ardent spirits. Fire separates the molecules, giving them distance and energy, making the frantic dance of escape. As the necromancer conjures spirits from the earth, so the moonshiner conjures up whiskey, *uisge beatha:* the water of life. It is, in short, backwoods alchemy. Boiling below and cooling above, lifting the living waters.

The four ancient elements are all necessary: earth from which the corn and barley rise, water to break down the grains and sugars, fire to bring the mash to boiling, and an airy essence rising into the cooling coils. Condensed to liquid form, the fifth element—the quintessence—appears: a droplet hanging from the copper worm's lip, a perfect elongated sphere, then—too heavy— it falls to join its brothers. Then another begins to form. Running it twice through my stovetop still, I converted five gallons of mash into a half pint of white lightning, the shine of the moon itself captured in a jar.

On a night when Eileen isn't home, I get out my Mason jar of homemade whiskey and put the Louvin Brothers on the stereo. The track that hits me hardest as I swig down my homemade rocket fuel is "The Kneeling Drunkard's Plea." It's sickly sentimental, the only song I know that rhymes "old country church" with "stagger and lurch." A boozer comes just one day too late to say goodbye to his dying mother. "Lord, have mercy on me," is this kneeling drunkard's plea. Well-lubricated, longing to conjure back the feeling of the big sings—powerful, relentless, raw with happiness—I kneel at the side of my bed, fold my hands to pray and sing along with Ira and Charlie, as they beg for forgiveness.

The song ends with the drunkard kneeling on the ground and the singers proclaiming their certainty "that God from heaven looked down." But as I rise from my knees, I think of what a neo-pagan friend of mine said once. "A prayer is just a spell tricked out in religious drag; and a spell was originally music: incantation, chanting, song."

HOLLIS HOUSE OF HORROR

It's the day after Halloween and I have a strong, strange, feeling about the sign we just passed. "Hollis House of Horror." I turn around and head off the main highway, along a winding road into the cold November sunset.

It's not very far, but that mile or two takes me back about a hundred years. The House of Horror was probably built at the turn of the last century. It's all raw gray wood, up on tottering piles of red stone. Boards are peeling off. The windows are broken out, boarded up, or hung with burlap for curtains. The roof is rusted iron sheeting.

But this relic of old, lost times, is layered over with teenage self-terrorizing schlock. Local kids had known about the abandoned farmer's shack forever and this year they moved in to make it their Halloween horror house.

Outside, the main ingredient is black plastic sheeting, flapping walls to make a maze and spray-painted with various slogans and threats.

Redneck Revenge!

Death is coming, hell is moving. That's from **"Holy Manna,"** which was the song Kester led most often.

Hand of God has struck the hour. That's from Black Sabbath's "War Pigs."

In front is a makeshift ticket booth. The door it guards is locked. But going around back, I find easy entrance. The first room looks like a childish mock-slaughter site. Fake blood is spattered on the walls, on the pictures of Jesus hanging there, on the gutted furniture. Rubber monster masks lay on the floor like shed reptile skins.

Only twelve hours before, the place had been alive with screams, groans, imbecile laughter, and heavy metal bellowing. Now the place is silent. Walking carefully over the rotted floors, I go deeper, into the inner sanctum. More black plastic, more barely legible graffiti.

Spider Baby Bites.
Darkness Fire and Pain. (More Sacred Harp.)
Children of the Grave. (More Black Sabbath.)

I retreat and make my stand in the main murder-scene room. I know it's fake, a way for some teenagers to have some grisly fun and make a few dollars. But the combination of old and new is like nothing I've ever experienced. Two worlds are superimposed: old, crumbling Alabama poverty homestead and horror party atrocity zone.

Both worlds are empty now. The screams are silent and the backcountry people who'd actually lived here are long dead. No more zombies or vampires. No more hardscrabble dirt farmers too poor to have indoor plumbing or electricity.

The back porch is barely strong enough to hold my

weight, the boards all splintered, weak and sagging like hundred-year-old bones. Standing there, I get a better glimpse of the original owner's lives: the ruins of a mule pen like the skeleton of an extinct monster, concrete cistern to catch the rainwater, crumbling barn and ghostly corn crib, spectral outhouse. The sun is just at the horizon, smeared red-orange behind the hay fields. Not a car goes by the entire time I'm there.

I flee, crunching over the red dirt driveway. The black plastic, like abandoned flags of defeat, quivers in the wind. I didn't know it could get so cold in Alabama.

LUDDITES

I had to travel to southern Ohio (not Alabama) to meet real Luddites. I had to spend time with Quakers, old order Mennonites, and Amish (not Primitive Baptists) to taste the realness of archaic ways. You can sing tunes from two hundred years back, you can have fantasies of the clippy-clop horse and buggy good old days, but as long as you're living the high-tech life, then you're living in the now that lasts only a nanosecond. One of the reasons I love Sacred Harp is its strange relationship to time itself. While singing, the hours fly past. And years too: a blur of then and now and some day.

Eileen and I drove ten hours to attend the third Luddite Congress, organized by the Center for Plain Living. We'd heard about the event through their magazine, *Plain*, which was then still handset, letter by painstaking letter.

Say you're a Luddite and most Americans will either shy away as though you're a creepy cultist or dump a load of puzzled condescension. "How could an intelligent, educated person like you embrace such a ridiculous philosophy?" The term "Luddite" is often used as a weapon to dismiss or belittle. The image conjured up is a rage-filled, brainless destroyer of technology. Picture a caveman smashing a computer with a stone ax and you get a pretty good idea of the cliché.

But for the 350 self-styled Luddites who gathered in southern Ohio, this description couldn't have been more wrong-headed. For these folks, the term Luddite was neither a joke nor an embarrassment. They gathered from across the country to talk, to share meals, to pray, to encourage one another, but mostly to listen. The best definition I heard of Luddite is this simple: "All new technologies are guilty until proven innocent."

The organizers asked that no photos be taken during the sessions; a sketch artist worked much of the time, capturing his very subjective impressions of the events. There was no sound recording either. And the choice not to amplify the speeches had a curious effect; the audience got quieter when a speaker's voice flagged. For the hearing impaired there was an old-fashioned solution: the front benches were reserved for them. With hard wooden pews, bare white walls, high empty spaces, the huge 1878 Quaker meetinghouse was the perfect location for such a gathering.

When we told the couple who ran the Congress about Sacred Harp, they were intrigued and invited us back to their home, off the grid and off the map. I was struck by their strangely compelling choices about life. Horse and buggy, sawdust toilet, propane lights, Old Order Quaker clothing. We talked a lot about books—mostly books for children. As we were leaving, our host suggested that we sing for each other. So, Eileen and I sang **"Northfield"** from *The Sacred Harp*. Then the whole family (six kids aged twelve to one) gathered at the other end of the table and sang together a song for us. They did a second song and we replied with **"Wondrous Love."**

It felt both formal and intimate. It wasn't show-offy at all. Not amazing, not beautiful, but freely given and gratefully received. So, there were the little Quaker girls, barefoot, in long dresses with head-coverings, singing shyly for strangers. And there we were, welcome guests, saying goodbye.

They said they'd like it if we could come back another time and do a whole weekend of teaching. We agreed and returned a few months later. The group was far smaller. We didn't convene in the great meeting hall, but in one of the side rooms, where our voices wouldn't be swallowed in the heights above the balcony. The floor tilted heavily to one side and wooden benches were stiff and square. After the Sunday gathering for worship, the retreat group sang three songs for our hosts. It felt great to be myself in that huge space: loud and reedy and real.

A few Sacred Harp singers of the Quaker persuasion came from far off to help us out, and unlike at most sings or singing schools, we mixed in periods of silent meditation. Eileen chose phrases from some of the tunes to use for centering prayer and contemplation.

> *Sister spirit come away*
> *Now shall my inward joys arise*
> *Join in and help me to sing*
> *Vital spark of heavenly flame*

No blood atonement or fire of vengeance. These were Quakers, pacifists, people who refuse the sword and whose Sunday services were sometimes totally silent. Still, they joined in when it was time to let their voices loose.

Some of the attendees wore plain clothes and still used a horse and buggy. Most drove cars and were plugged into mainstream America. But for a couple of days, we could sing together a loud and boisterous "No!" to the degradations of modern American culture.

PARTING HAND

There's a prayer at the beginning of most big sings. Frequently I hear people asking God to grant "traveling mercies" to those who haven't arrived yet. Also, at the end of the day, there's a prayer to get everyone home safely. Usually, God is amenable to such requests.

The long road has always been part of the Sacred Harp tradition. All the way back to the beginning in the first decades of the nineteenth century, shaped note singers were known to travel great distances and stay overnight with people they barely knew, or on the hard cold ground.

The farthest I've driven for a one-day sing is five hundred miles round trip. Eight hours in the car for six hours of singing. Others though have far more endurance for the road, getting up well before dawn and not flopping into some borrowed bed until long after midnight.

By now, I've sung with perhaps a thousand others: from Canada to Mississippi, from Ohio to Boston. Some I know well, having enjoyed their hospitality, from roughing it to luxury. Others remain anonymous. If you don't sign up to lead, then nobody hears your name called and you may go away unknown. There are hundreds of singers whose voices joined with mine only once. They happened to travel farther than usual, like me on certain trips, and so our paths crossed for only a few hours.

In late afternoon, with the ghost of the lonesome road floating above the hollow square, I sense a touch of sadness. At the end of big sings there comes a time when everyone stands and sings goodbye with a handshake or hug. In many places the song is "Parting Hand," which tells of singers who "in sweetest union join," but then must bid farewell. As the sun is setting, only faint echoes remain. There's a solitude, a paradoxical quality of exile, of bereavement, that pervades the sound. The square breaks up and we're back on the road, heading home.

On our last trip down south, we stayed at a nineteenth century home. Nothing fancy—no pillars out front or stately moss-draped live oaks. This place had never been part of a big plantation. But out in the fields, maybe a half mile back, were the remains of a slave shack.

After the big singing at Mount Pisgah, we car-pooled back to our host's place. He was a kindly and decent man, opening his home to strangers from the North. He made no excuses nor brushed off his family's tainted history. Still, there it was, seen out his kitchen window every day.

As the sun was going down, I trekked out through the fields to the slave shack. Cotton had long ago been replaced by fast-growing pines for pulpwood. But these fields, where for decades black slaves and then white sharecroppers had labored, were still in cultivation. Corn maybe, soy or sorghum. I'm not sure. It was all stubble and hard-packed dirt when I ventured into the fields. The shack was mostly gone: a chimney made of rocks and a rough foundation.

I stood a while in the remains of the hovel, soaking in the silence and shadows. I had a sense, walking back, that I would not be returning to Alabama. But I had no holier-than-thou moment, no big revelation standing in that ruin. It was sadness I felt, a deep grieving knowledge that I would soon be making my farewells.

That night, some of us sang at our host's dining room table. We did **"Nearer, My God, to Thee,"** and "The Old Rugged Cross," which had been my father's favorite hymn. As the final song faded into silence, I knew I'd never see Kester again. The guy who'd given him a ride needed to be heading back. Kester got up, put his hand on my shoulder, and said goodbye without saying a word. I went out with him to the porch, then watched him vanish into the darkness. Two headlights came on, poking holes in the misty night air, and the tires crunched slowly down the gravel drive. I stood there until the last trace of the car had disappeared.

AND MUST THE DEAD ARISE?

I stood alone on Cobb's Hill under lead-blue autumnal skies in a steady rising wind. A reservoir takes up most of the hilltop, with a Greek revival pumphouse standing guard on the west end and a seven-foot-tall iron picket fence all the way around. To one side stands a radio mast with a dozen microwave dishes pointed in all directions.

On the north edge of the hill's steep incline, I looked out over Rochester and sang into the cold, groaning wind.

> How long, dear Savior, O how long,
> Shall this bright hour delay?
> Fly swift around, ye wheels of time,
> And bring the promised day.

And singing these three-hundred-year-old words of Isaac Watts, I wondered if I was taunting the divine, trying to goad him into returning right then and there. But if countless end-time true-believers couldn't bring the return of Jesus, then surely my lone voice could have no effect on the Great Timeline of God.

William Miller had determined, through careful study of the Bible, that October 22, 1844 would be the date of Christ's return. At the height of the Millerite frenzy, fifty thousand souls waited together for the end of time. They gathered to listen, to pray, and to sing the old hymns of Christ's return.

> From the third heaven where God resides,
> That holy happy place
> The new Jerusalem comes down,
> Adorned with shining grace.

I climbed Cobb's Hill on a much later October 22 and looked out over the city as the Millerites had, waiting for the rapturous end.

Thousands had gathered on this drumlin just above the Rochester wide-waters of the Grand Erie Canal. Thousands stood expectant, longing for the joyous thunderclap of jubilee. Christ the bridegroom, they were convinced, was coming back that cold October day to sweep up in his loving arms the true church, his true bride.

Miller claimed that in over a thousand small towns and cities, in villages and hamlets and crossroads scattered across the region, the Adventist passions burned brightly. And at the time when the entire population of the U.S. was only 19,000,000, there were almost a million of those who were "skeptically expectant."

Miller's prophesy struck a loud, ringing chord with the God-mad American population, like a great hand sweeping across the strings of a vast heavenly harp.

Reluctant at first, Miller merely wanted others to understand the secret truth he'd discovered. But his words set the land ablaze and soon he was traveling with a tent large enough to hold a thousand listeners. And his services had all the emotional fury of Great Awakening camp meetings: new converts shouting and wailing, falling to the ground in trances, barking like dogs and speaking in unknown human tongues.

Legend had it that many had sold their earthly goods and given up all claims to this world. These fervent pilgrims in white robes came thronging to the top of Cobb's Hill, expecting this world of woe and travail to be transformed in an instant. What tears were cried, what fond good-byes were spoken, we'll never know. What were the infirmities and afflictions that these folk wanted to shed like ragged old clothes? How many parents imagined themselves in a New Jerusalem embracing their dead children?

Instead of Jesus returning to gather up his wild-eyed Yankee religionists, 1844 saw the far less spectacular, and far more satisfying, first appearance of *The Sacred Harp*. At the end of the longed-for day, Jesus still hadn't come back. This non-event is called by church historians The Great Disappointment. Some say Miller had been close but missed the target by a week: on October 15, Nietzsche (who would at times declare himself to be the Antichrist) had been born.

Below me I saw the city of Rochester. Not a single building was visible that had stood there on the day of Christ's expected appearance. The Wheel of Time had turned: years and decades and centuries. The city below me would've been unrecognizable to the Millerites, yet the sky and the seasons were the same.

William Miller's followers had seen those same scarlet spikes, mottled bronze and gold, ochre and umber, trees stretching away in the north to Lake Ontario and in the south to the undulating blue-haze of the Bristol Hills. A few steeple spires had poked up from the landscape in 1844, but those churches are gone. Now it's Xerox and Kodak, banks, and monolithic corporate towers.

As I waited, shivering and alone, the wind picked up even more fiercely. I heard a quaking rumble and for just a flash, I thought, "This is it." I was skeptically expectant, imagining what the Millerites must have imagined: great hosts of true believers sweeping into the sky.

The wind roared and rumbled through the iron spikes of the picket fence and I looked back at myself at sixteen years old, reading pop-cult prophesy about Christ returning as a thief in the night to carry away to heaven all his beloved.

Hearing the long echo of fear, I remembered the millennial madness that had dragged me weeping to God as a teenager. (That is: I'd read the best-selling *Late Great Planet Earth* and had fallen for its sloppy, sleazy prophesies about the end of the world.) Now, afraid to hear the last trumpet blast, I ran for my car and sped away.

A few days after my Cobb's Hill foray, deep in the library stacks, I found a tattered, ribbon-wrapped copy of *The Millennial Harp*. The Millerites had sung from this book as they waited for the Final Day. They sang until their voices went hoarse, then silent. Secret and alone in the library, I took up the song again.

How will my heart endure
The terrors of that day,
When earth and heaven before His face,
Astonished shrink away?

And will the Judge descend
And must the dead arise?
And not a single soul escape
His all-discerning eyes?

BEAR CREEK

On the winter solstice, I go east along the lake shore with my friend James, the mad surfer. He and other holy-men brave the ice on Lake Ontario in the subfreezing depths of winter. In wet suits, they skid their boards into the churning purple-black water, past wave-gnawed crusts of ice, past the barely submerged rocks, and head out to catch the waves. Mild insanity, strong devotion, and courage: all three are needed for the rites of the ride.

North Coast December winds, whipping up tendrils of snow. The darkening tail of late afternoon. Out beyond the Wayne County line, past the grim silhouette of the nuclear power plant, glimpsed through the barren apple orchards. Out to Bear Creek, which is high and flowing hard today, pouring its inky iridescence into the lake.

I bring along a recording, over a half a century old. It's "Bear Creek," one of the most raucous of Sacred Harp tunes. James has it blasting in his car as we pull into the boat launch parking lot.

> Lord when Thou didst ascend on high,
> Ten thousand angels filled the sky,
> Those heav'nly guards around Thee wait
> Like chariots that attend Thy state.

"Bear Creek" goes back two hundred years and is usually sung with plenty of foot-stomping and the volume turned all the way to max.

James says he can use the angelic guardians at the Bear Creek outlet, because the shore there is a real hazard. Other guys have already wrecked boards and gotten cut up on the rocks and broken blades of ice.

No other surfers have come to the secret spot that day, just a thirtyish couple enjoying the aphrodisiac powers of the sunset, clinging, making out in the wild wind. They let each other go and give me a sheepish greeting as I take their spot on the height above the creek's outlet.

Sealed head to toe in his sleek black superhero suit, James paddles out through the waves. I stand and watch the solitary rite from a little promontory on the shore.

A woman appears. No car—she must've come from one of the nearby cottages.

She gives me a quick glance, but we both know better than to speak. I turn away, to give her privacy just as the sun and sky make their ancient crimson fusion. She stands facing the west with her arms out in a reverential pose, as the Children of the Sun (German proto-hippies) were wont to do on pagan holy days: hailing the solar self-immolation.

Staring out at big black icy water, I think about my ancestors, who all came from northern Europe. The

Prussians were on the Baltic and the Scots were on the North Sea. They came to Rochester, which is on the easternmost of the Great Lakes. It's no coincidence that I like it here: big water and strong winters.

This is a sacred moment: a surf-sadhu in a rubber Batman suit trying to catch a wave, a strange woman making her pagan Salute to the Solstice, and me looking at the greatness of the lake, bundled up against the wind.

The western dusk-glow isn't spectacular tonight. No fiery sky-battles, no obvious armies of ten thousand angels hovering that evening. I do not see the Lord ascending high, just Ontario's broken black mirror of the nightening sky.

But James rises to catch some waves. He manages to avoid the rocks and the knife-edges of ice. His chariot-board eventually brings him back to shore safely, as the sun worshiper finishes her silent devotions, and disappears.

THE SECRET SCHOOLROOM

About once a week, Eileen and I sang together, just the two of us in the living room. Tenor and treble are enough to give the feeling, and I sometimes poked out a few bass notes on the piano. Or we sat at the kitchen table where we've eaten our meals together for forty years (and where I'm writing this book) and caught the reverb off the wall.

Far better was when we went to visit another couple—alto and bass—and made hours of music in their Secret Schoolroom. Dev and Rivka are the age our kids would've been, if we'd decided to go that route. When they first came to the Rochester local, they were good musicians, but had only done Sacred Harp a few times, back in their Bard College days. I wouldn't use the word "teaching" to describe what went on, but there was definitely a feel of passing something along. Stories of our sojourns south, tunes we associated with singers from the North who'd died, bits of traditional practice that we'd picked up over the years. (For instance, there's a spot in **"Wondrous Love"** where some tenors jump in early. I learned that from Jeff Sheppard, one of the standard bearers on Sand Mountain, and was pleased when I heard Dev doing it too.)

Early on, I went to see Rivka do a show at the Bug Jar, the bastion of punk rock in Rochester. I'd played on that stage a half dozen times (once in a band that included two theremins and a fire breather). I went to hear Rivka, to cheer on the home team, standing in the back of the dank, dark, cold, dirty room, and left as soon as her set was over.

Dev and Rivka's condominium was part of a retrofitted school building. Passing through the modern living room and kitchen, we traveled back fifty years. There was a room left largely untouched, with scuffed hardwood floor, the original blackboards with wooden chalk trays, cast iron radiators hanging ten feet off the ground and pebbled glass skylights.

The building was a Spanish colonial revival with a red tiled roof, totally wrong for winter-ravaged Rochester, yet exactly right too, a charming oddity. It was built in 1913 to replace a school that burned down. All on one level, it was designed so that every classroom had an exit directly outside. When it was rehabbed in 1980, the interior was divided up so that certain condos got a portion of the lost places, unseen and inadmissible from outside.

Dev and Rivka got the space that I dubbed the Secret Schoolroom. It had no windows, but the ceiling was entirely double-layered glass, fogged and obscured by dirt, but still letting in some sunshine. Over the years they lived there, the blackboard acquired a dense palimpsest of chalked images and messages. I wouldn't call it graffiti. The board was more like a guest book: with cartoons, sigils, gnomic sayings, schematics, and musical fragments.

Entering the room, it was easy for me to imagine decades of school kids spilling their detritus and sticky goo on the floors. But Dev and Rivka made the room very much their own. A lot of Rivka's art was tacked up on the bulletin boards, including a large portrait of Nick Cave, who always looked over at me with big, baleful eyes as we sang. A pagan altar to St. Bridget, a washing machine, an electric guitar, and keyboard had their places in the schoolroom. The radiators, I learned, were so far off the floor so little kids wouldn't burn their hands.

The room had a fine ring for singing, and we sounded pretty damned good there, the four of us. We ate some pizza or pasta and a couple times played a Lovecraft-themed board game ("Arkham Horror," in which everyone always loses and descends into madness and damnation). Then one of us would say, "You want to sing?" and we'd retire to the Secret Schoolroom for a couple of hours of doomy, happy, dreary, joyful noise. We'd go until one of us said, "I've only got one more song in me," and then after a bit of small talk, we were on our way home.

One night in the Secret Schoolroom, we got talking about tears. All of us said we'd cried at Sacred Harp sings. Dev told us about a client of his who'd committed suicide not long before and singing **"Granville"** at our all-day regional had really opened up something inside him. That is, he couldn't keep on singing for a while, going off to be alone with his grief. The rest of us had less dramatic stories, but we all knew what he meant when he said, "That one really messed me up."

This was just for us—Eileen and I, Dev, and Rivka. Not just friendship, though that was certainly part of it, and not just a couple hours of good strong singing. We were a quartet, the bare bones of Sacred Harp: bass, alto, treble and tenor. We all knew our parts well or could learn them readily. We all had the same level of devotion. This really mattered: a kind of intimacy: four voices exposed in a secret special space.

We sang there eighteen times. I know that for sure, because after the first sing I attended, I began a log, and have written down every single time we've ever been part of a Sacred Harp event. Large or small—it didn't matter—I wrote down where and when.

I loved visiting the venerable southern churches. Singing in a beautiful edifice in Manhattan was also a treat. The Mennonite church where we still sing is a place near to my heart. (I helped design, pay for, and raise the building. When the hard wood flooring was delivered, I was the only one around, so I carried a couple of tons of finished wood—bundle by bundle—into the building.) But none of those locations had the same feel as the Secret Schoolroom, with just the four of us present. With dining room chairs in a little square, with their first child nearby in his toddler corral, we were a quartet.

Much to my delight, Dev and Rivka agreed to host larger singings at their place. We'd hold annual Saturday regional singings at the Mennonite Church. Then the next day people were invited to the 5S: Second Sunday Secret Schoolroom Sing. We didn't publish the address, giving it the feel of a clandestine rendezvous. You had to come on Saturday to get directions. The group was smaller there, more relaxed. The room felt pleasantly crowded with only thirty or so singers. We didn't bring in food. Take-out pizza was fine for lunch. The hollow square was made up of a hodgepodge of folding chairs, dining room furnishings, and whatever else singers brought to sit on. Making music in someone's home, especially deep inside the space, brought the group together with a special quality of closeness in a way that no big sing ever did for me.

Then Dev's job took them back to New York City, they rented out the condo and the schoolroom was no more. When we said goodbye, I felt something die inside me.

We kept in touch, by electronic means, by phone and by that most wonderful of nineteenth century technologies: the U.S. Mail. Rivka sent me a postcard showing Sid Vicious at Max's Kansas City in 1978. One of the fans in the picture looks eerily like Eileen as a college girl. She was not interested in punk rock, then or now, and never would have gone to see Sid. But I liked the idea of her doppelganger hanging out at the scummy club where a thousand punk bands had played. In reply, I sent Rivka a hand-painted postcard from the 1940s, touting a hideous hotel bar called the Purple Tree. My message: "Greetings from the past, where everyone is old and drunk."

THE SHENANDOAH HARMONY

In the last two centuries, there have been dozens of shape note books. Almost all of them are long out of print and largely forgotten. *The Shenandoah Harmony*, however, is the new gospel plow, digging a deep and rich furrow. Containing five hundred long-lost and recently found songs, this new book came on strong as serious competition for *The Sacred Harp*.

It's a much more adventurous collection and is already causing much worry for the Deep South traditionalists. The compilers dug far into obscure sources, some of the songs literally appearing in print for the first time since before the Civil War. There are some new ones too, greatest hits by modern Northerners such as Neely Bruce, Hal Kunkel, and Judy Hauff. The Shenandoah committee had also gone out of its way to avoid lyrics that targeted American Indians for insult ("No more the war-whoop be heard") or were overtly antisemitic ("in spite of envious Jews.")

Eileen and I had followed the development of this new book, singing off xeroxes in the early stages, mostly to support our friends in Virginia and Pennsyltucky. But when the finished collection appeared and we attended our first all-day Shenandoah sing, I was struck hard, the way I had been years before by my first taste of the Sacred Harp.

"Madness," "In Evil Long," "Day of Judgment," "A Doleful Sound," and "Night of the Grave," not one but two tunes called "Despair," "Thorn" and "Thorny Desert," "Sons of War," "Gravity," "Bondage" and "Buzzard's Glory": these titles go right up to the edge, and then over. One of my favorites is called "Heck," the closest shape note gets to the straight-eight hammer beat of the Ramones. Making an overt nod to shape note's pagan ancestry, there's also "Venus," "Rome," and "Morpheus."

At Bethlehem, PA, I led "Heck," and "Glory Shone Around" (the most clamorous Christmas song I know). *The Shenandoah Harmony* is even more "dread"—to use the word in the way the Rastafarians do—than *The Sacred Harp*. More minor tunes, more weird harmonies, in some cases a more primitive—or primal—sound.

After the sing, John del Re led us to a nearby graveyard to gaze on a most passing strange obelisk: about twenty feet tall, a perfectly smooth spiral with a cone on top: a cross between extruded soft-serve ice cream and a huge kundalini phallus made of gleaming stone. In the dusky background, beyond the coiled granite death/life-prong, stood the smokestack ruins of Bethlehem Steel.

Standing in the shadow of the great obscene grave shaft, a young woman we'd never met before asked Eileen and I how long we'd been together. I suppose she noticed that we got along well. Yes, she was a nameless stranger, but we'd just spent six hours yelling with her about doom and glory. "Forty years," I said. She said her parents had been together about that long because they were good at avoiding painful truths. I told her we headed straight in, and usually came out the other side better for it.

So: much big strong sound, mystic American madness, and later I got to again experience the delights of magic meat, aka genuine barbecued roadkill. We went to a social afterward, at a farmhouse just east of Butztown and Hecktown, PA. There, I was pleased to find, was a crockpot full of venison harvested off a dead deer. It had been hit by a car and wandered, dying, onto Farmer Dan's land. He said that if the car hits a deer at too high a rate of speed, the internal organs explode. So, roadkill from winding back roads is best. "Slow killed, slow cooked," his wife added. "That's the best."

Typically, there's a big crock of pulled pork at shaped note meals. Kester's well-guarded recipe was famous north and south, his version of the body and blood of Christ all mixed together with sweet and smokey sauce. But BBQ venison (especially from a deer that dragged itself onto a singer's land just so it could be harvested and transformed into a tasty dish for faraway singers) seems to me more auspicious.

JESUS, THEN MOLOCH

I was chairing the New York State convention again. We gathered this time at Tay House on Cobbs Hill, a rustic lodge named after the Tay River in Scotland. It was the first time we'd used this space, and it turned out to be perfect for the convention. The scuffed linoleum floor and hundred-year-old raw wood walls threw back just the right amount of reverb.

A narrow stairway led to the room's west gallery. I climbed the steps after a few hours of singing, to look down on the group. About forty people remained. By Sunday afternoon, our convention usually starts to lose bodies and momentum. But it still sounded fine. The group seemed warm, comfortable, happy.

A new guy—wearing scarves and exuding patchouli fumes—had shown up earlier and stayed the whole time. Though he sang not a single note, that day his tears flowed. He listened and wondered at the phenomenon. "I can't believe this thing exists," he said to me when he came to our next month's local sing. A much smaller group, loose and friendly, we welcomed Harold and he threw all he had into the sound. His first time actually singing with us was at our hundredth anniversary: a hundred times we'd sung at the Mennonite meeting house I'd helped to design, pay for, and build. (Just before we lay down the flooring in the main room, I drew shape notes on the bare concrete. Only I know the location of this secret sweet spot.)

Harold had spent the whole convention in the bass section. But he was clearly a tenor. With this revelation, Harold insisted on a place at my right hand, where he could best hear and feel my voice. As he got stronger, sitting beside me time after time, I felt the strange exchange of energy. His voice from my mouth—my voice from his body. Half my age, the frontman from a well-tattooed "immersive performance" group called the Velvet Noose, he brought passion and rawness to the group.

He was the same age I'd been when I first entered the sanctified precincts of the Sacred Harp. Sitting next to him, running my finger under the notes to help him out, I got some vicarious wonder and buzz. It was all new to him, all rich and strange, as it had been for me years before.

In some ways, we're as different as can be. I'd been reading music since I was ten years old. When Harold first opened his *Sacred Harp*, he couldn't make any sense of what was on the page. He's an extrovert, loaded with trendy tattoos. For all my yelling and helling, I'm really an introvert, and my skin is still pristine. He grew up on the far side of the continent and moved around a lot. I've never lived more than a half hour's drive from the spot where I was born.

But there are times when it feels we share some very significant DNA and mojo. The main evidence of this link is our lives in performance art. He does, and I did, dozens of weird shows for adventurous, too-hip scenesters. My group was called Health and Beauty (and our unpaid roadies were Health and Beauty Aids). I gave up amusing and freaking-out strangers exactly at the time I discovered Sacred Harp. Harold is very much still at it: creating "sound-baths" with a battery of gongs, working with huge puppets and self-described ecstatic dancers.

The first time I saw him perform, he and his troupe wore grotesque masks, struck hieratic postures, pounded on drums, and chanted endlessly the name of a Canaanite fire god. An hour before, we'd been in the Secret Schoolroom, singing about Jesus and his ten thousand charms. Now Harold's group appeared to be summoning up the ancient god Moloch, to whom children were once sacrificed.

Immersed in the Velvet Noose, as at a big sing, time seemed to slow, then run backwards. For a while, I floated in Harold's bizarre performance limbo. Then the performers withdrew, the oppressive electronic muzak started up again, and people started chattering. The spell was broken and the clocks went forward again. No horrible deities had appeared and no children were burned on bloody altars.

While I'd never taken part in such a rite, there were some echoes from my earlier performance art days. The Velvet Noose employs elaborate costumes and stagecraft; Health and Beauty made far more use of power tools, free jazz, and fake blood. Still, both groups often pushed at the boundaries of reason with crazed music and distressing stage antics. For me, Sacred Harp wasn't a replacement for Health and Beauty, but the next step. I always hated performing on stage, and yet I kept going back. Discovering shape note singing, I was free of bars and clubs, with their smoke, bad lighting, and hipper-than-thou denizens. I could still yell my head off, and there was plenty of blood: though salvific, not theatrical.

THE SPIRIT ROOM

As I'd hoped, Dev and Rivka returned from New York City and moved back into their Secret Schoolroom condo. With their voices added back to our group, we had new life, new power, new-old happiness.

Harold's presence among us, and a new guy from Kentucky, made a big difference. Jason had the experience and academic qualifications, but he took his time, listening month after month, observing our group's particular ways before entering the square. When he did, it was with no pompous PhD affectations. He banged the air with his fist, making a very distinctive, propulsive beat. He understood that a choir and a hollow square are radically different musical organisms.

Our local sing picked up momentum—some younger people, lots of tunes from *The Shenandoah Harmony*, and then an event that stretched us out of the usual safety of the square. Eight of us sang for an hour at the Spirit Room, the same place I'd first experienced the Velvet Noose.

It's a bar, devoted to spiritualism, all sorts of outré music, goth décor, and general booga-booga bizarrerie.

And there we sang about the blood of Christ while looking at nineteenth century magician posters and voodoo chachkas. Eileen gave up counting skulls at two dozen. Our octet consisted of three performance-art weirdos (Harold, Rivka, and I), a fiddler, a bass player in a power-punk band, a children's choir director, Dev the psychologist, and Eileen (who came directly to the Spirit Room from a five-day Buddhist retreat.)

I was strongly averse to performing Sacred Harp on a stage. The singing is supposed to be just for the people who come and invest their voices in the greater din. Yet this night we put on a show, not a communal event, and I surprised myself by accepting it as okay, probably because the place is such a freaky venue. The regulars try so hard to be hip, yet our audience seemed genuinely engaged. And all the skulls and black candles and hoodoo kitsch made me feel welcome. No pictures of Jesus, even though we were singing about him and his blood.

Though we weren't really trying to raise the dead or get a message from the other side, we went heavy on the doom and drear, driving our voices really hard. However, in that space, there was a more-than-usual element of necromancy in the singing. The spirits want music. The dead can still hear us and we can hear them.

Among the Primitive Baptists, there are only two postmortem options. The preachers proclaim it and *The Sacred Harp* spells it out, voicing the hope that we might "escape hell and fly to heaven." Yes, we sing a lot of heaven-songs, and get a goodly dose of hell too. But I became increasingly sure there was a third path. If the ancestors are far, far away—walking the golden streets in eternal day, or lying at "hell's dark door"—how then can they join us in sweet union?

I have no interest in theological argument. It's not belief that moves me, but experience. And after years in the hollow square, I didn't doubt what I felt, in my blood and bones and deepest brain flesh. The dead are still alive, in an interzone beyond time and space. Music dissolves the line that separates us from those who came before.

Some Christians condemn the blues and hillbilly bawling (and the offspring of their moonlight mating: rock and roll), asking, "Why does the devil have all the best music?" I say this is a damn fool question, and assert here a far better one: "Why do the Christians have all the best hymns?"

We finished at the Spirit Room with "Doomsday."

> Nature, in wild amaze,
> Her dissolution mourns;
> Blushes of blood the moon deface;
> The sun to darkness turns.
> The living look with dread,
> The frighted dead arise,
> Start from the monumental bed,
> And lift their ghastly eyes.

THE TRAVELER COMES HOME

Initiating new friends and out of town guests into the arcana of Mount Hope Cemetery, I usually take them to see the monument I call The Traveler. Bigger than life size, he reclines at the top of a hill, with water jug and scallop shell (to prove that he'd returned from his holy land pilgrimage). He supports his head with one hand, the other rests on his staff. Bearded, bald, and robed, he is also sometimes referred to as The Weary Pilgrim.

Mount Hope is a charmed and charming place, designed to be a park for the living as well as an earthen bed for the dead. For nearly two hundred years, visitors have come here to enjoy the sinuous trails, overgrown ravines, funeral monuments (both grand and paltry), lost corners where few venture to go, and stone stairways that lead upwards to nothing. I have sojourned here dozens of times, and always I discover some new shadowy nook or bizarre bit of statuary.

My mother's parents, her sister, and her grandparents are buried in Mount Hope. My father's grandparents are also interred here. There are notables—Frederick

Douglass and Susan B. Anthony—whose graves are visited by thousands every year. And there are three hundred and fifty thousand less famous others, which is greater than the population of Rochester, the city that gave birth to, and now surrounds and feeds, the cemetery.

Today, I've brought Harold and our mutual friend Steve to this Beautiful City of the Dead. Today, as is often my habit, I lead them to the hilltop where the Traveler rests in sad revery. And it is here that we sing from *The Sacred Harp* in rough unison.

> Do not I love Thee, O my Lord?
> Behold my heart and see.

We sing for ourselves and each other, and we sing for the third of a million dead who surround us, listening.

After a long circuitous wander, we make our descent to where we'd parked, in the shadow of the original crematory. As long as I could remember, this gothic crypto-chapel has been closed. But we see workers moving in and out today. Built in 1862, with the crematorium added in 1912 (the steeple is hollow and acted as a smokestack), the building is not just on the side of a hill, but actually extends underground.

Steve says, "Let's see if we can get inside."

I'm hesitant, not in the mood to haggle with the construction crew. But Steve pulls out a twenty-dollar bill and says, "I'm an old white man. I can go wherever I want." This isn't a thoughtless brag, but a statement of fact. We're gray-haired, well-spoken, and I'm carrying a nineteenth century hymnal. What's the worst that three archaic music nerds can do? The twenty is not necessary. The worker we speak with is a bit puzzled, but just shrugs and tells us not to go too deeply inside.

Careful to stay in the safe zone, on the plywood path that leads into the dank underground darkness, we aim our voices at the high arched south end and let rip with our plaintive call.

> But O I long to soar
> Far from the sphere of mortal joys.

"This one's for Kester." I'd gotten the message just that morning. Kester Vines had gone to play on the golden harp of heaven. Neither Steve nor Harold had met him, but they'd heard plenty of my stories. Moonshine, pig meat, coon dogs, the Louvin Brothers, and "singing hoard." Yes, I remember him well and can evoke his spirit by singing his favorite songs, but with his death my most vital link to the Old Sacred Harp South is broken.

The crematory's echoes have a perfect decay, just long enough to soak into our brains and hearts. Our voices fill the space, and with each inbreath, our bodies are filled with the musty subterranean funk blended with the tang of fresh lumber. We thank the workers, and exit, carrying music—heard and unheard—back into the sunlight.

SINGING IN THE HEART OF THE EARTH

On the way to a sing in the Shenandoah Valley of Virginia, Eileen and I stop to visit our friend Hal. He suggests that we spend the afternoon at one of the local tourist attractions: Indian Caverns.

The giftshop there is like a cross between a cold war bomb shelter and a spruced-up hobbit hole. Next to it, the actual entrance is even more charming and pathetic. Thick shoulders of concrete and a massive door give the look of a mountainside bank vault. And to make our visit perfect, an all-day drizzle means that we're the only visitors.

Inside the cave, everything is all curves and bends and sloping slimy floors. Our guide does some of his standard canned patter. He points out the Frozen Niagara, a shining bubbling sheet of flowstone. Farther in, we see the Giant's Hall, and Indian carvings of highly questionable origin. (They look to me like the scrawl of drunken frat boys.)

The reach of the cave is slowly being pushed back. Here and there, we see evidence of volunteer spelunkers who come in at night to worm their way into crevasses, pulling out handfuls of reddish mud, just to see where the little side-channels go.

The whole time we're underground, I'm breathless, sure that we'll never get out. As we penetrate the narrowing chambers, questions gnaw at me: "Are you crazy? Why did you agree to do this?"

Neither Hal nor Eileen notice anything wrong. But the deeper we go, the more powerful becomes the sense of isolation, and the heavier becomes the weight of all that earth over my head.

Hal asks our guide if we might sing in the depths. It seems a bit odd, but we appear to be harmless nuts, bringing along our *Sacred Harps*, in hopes that we could test out the cave's acoustics, and our courage.

The guide is a pretty relaxed guy, and as it turns out a music history major too. So, he shrugs and says, "Sure." And at the deepest spot in the dripping, fifty-degree cave, with hibernating bats hanging near, he shuts out all the lights and we let it rip, singing from memory.

One hundred and twenty feet underground, the blackness is absolute. The feeling is overpowering: enveloped in ringing stone, ancient harmonies, and waves of claustrophobia. Though I crouch close to the other two, all I have to hang onto is their voices. Hal sings bass, Eileen does the high harmony, and I have the melody, pushing my voice as hard as it will go.

We wail **"Save, Mighty Lord"** and I think of miners lost in utter darkness, sure to die, raising a song to drive back the overpowering fear. I breathe in their loneliness and my self-inflicted doom.

I've felt this before, dozens of times: the heart-spasm cold surge of a panic attack. Deep breathing is usually helpful, but singing turns out to be even better to relieve the pressurized waves of dread. A few tunes, as loud as I can sing, with a few gasps here and there, and the panic retreats.

Then come the echoes and—for us—the return of light as our guide flips a switch. It's a rebirth ritual: baptism out of blackness.

Deeper into the cavern, in a narrow snaking passageway, our guide says, "Listen to this." He sings a low note, which makes the whole chamber resonate. Certain man-made rooms have sweet spots and keys they like best. But the living stone here rings, making real four-part harmony.

Hal finds the pitch (A flat) and we sing **"Do not I love thee, O my Lord?"** with the whole air space reverberating. **"Behold my heart and see."** We sing, and the cave—the earth itself holding us—sings with us.

Our last echoes die and we head upward. Emerging into the daylight, I feel the last of the panic recede. I can breathe freely again: restored to the middle world between heaven and hell, released and reborn.

MEMORIAL LESSON #3

September 2 is my birthday. And on this day, the core of my local Sacred Harp group gathered to sing in honor of the living and the dead.

I've decided on the spot where my so-called ashes will be scattered. I've come once again to Mount Hope Cemetery, the Beautiful City of the Dead, to locate the place where my six pounds of pale gray bone meal will be given back to the earth. Much as I love graveyards and grave monuments, my body will not be buried and there will be no stone marker. While giving a private tour of Mount Hope to an out-of-town filmmaker, telling them about local spiritualists and mystics of the fourth dimension, I realized that from certain vantage points in the cemetery, my birthplace—Strong Memorial Hospital—can be seen. The revelation came in a gentle flash: my mortal remains will be returned to the earth in this place, coming full circuit, from birth to death.

After cremation, there will be about a gallon of me left, mostly bone. Whoever remains after the fire and the funeral is hereby enjoined to give back to the ancestors the calcium phosphate sand that once was my skeleton.

My mother's parents and grandparents are buried in Mount Hope. At the Methodist church they attended, their songs were restrained, uninspired, wearisome at times. Still, they sang, and a lifetime later I brought their hymnal to their grave site. While I make no claim to literal shape note ancestors, there are ten songs in the Methodist hymnal that appear also in *The Sacred Harp*. With new harmonies added a hundred years ago, the arrangements are rather bland. Instead of these white bread arrangements, we sang on the anniversary of my birth much older versions of these songs, reaching back, across time and space.

I chose songs often done at more formal Memorial Lessons, and also asked my sextet of friends to make suggestions. "Farewell Anthem" was ragged, but none the less beautiful. "White" contains these words:

> I'm a long time trav'ling here below
> To lay this body down.
> Ye fleeting charms of earth farewell,
> Your springs of joy are dry;
> My soul now seeks another home,
> A brighter world on high.

I'd brought a photo of Janet, my mother's sister, who died at age four and is buried alongside her parents. I told stories of my great grandfather (working in a coal mine, and then the county prison, smoking cigars), my grandfather (Cadillac, suit and tie, more cigars).

And I recollected singers who were no longer with us. We sang **"Cusseta,"** and I described Allen Fannin's funeral.

I told them about Old Ron and how he loved "The Better Land." We did "Long Sought Home" after I talked about the visit of Father Frank X (the Bat-Priest) as Eileen and I sat with her sister on her last day of earthly life. We sang "Holy Manna," and I told my friends about Kester and how he had blessed me by saying that I sang *hoard*.

It had only been a few years since I'd been to the family grave site, but in the interim a new mausoleum had been erected a short distance away: an Egyptian revival pyramid. While hardly on the scale of the more famous pharaonic tombs, this one is remarkably large for an American cemetery (with room for eight full burial crypts) and is made of rainbow granite. In bright sunlight it glows with a subtle wave pattern of gold, green, flesh pink, black, and crimson.

Following an invisible arrow from the pyramid to my ancestors' grave, and then continuing across the cemetery, I saw (with no surprise) that it pointed to the maternity ward in Strong Memorial Hospital, where I was born.

After we sang, Jack and Danielle gave us bottles of cider freshly made from their own apple trees. I had brought garlic from my garden for the others to take home. Nathan sped off on his bike, while not quite as stylish as Bat-Priest, still looking rather like a superhero with his silver Hermes helmet. Rivka and Dev went with us to the pyramid after the others had gone, and we sat a while soaking in the Egyptomania birthday radiation.

Rivka noticed that at the peak of the monument is a translucent pyramid. This was supposedly put in place to allow in sunlight. But as Rivka pointed out, it gives the pyramid a subtle Illuminati finishing touch. Earlier, I'd called "Amsterdam," one of the hymns sung by my ancestors a hundred years back. Dev had asked about the words, which I'm convinced are far more hermetic than Christian. There's no Jesus in the song, but the mystic heavens are evoked.

> Sun and moon and stars decay
> Rise my soul and haste away.

The ancient pyramids, some adepts have conjectured, were not built to hold souls, but to shoot them back into the heavens whence they'd come. The stone pinnacles were aimed at certain stars, which were thought to be the birthplace of souls. Though some say this modern pyramid is just a million-dollar piece of kitsch, I wonder if it may have been designed—as the ancient Egyptians and the writers of *The Sacred Harp* hoped—to send the soul back to its place of origin.

> Rivers to the ocean run.
> Fire ascending seeks the sun.
> So a soul that's born of God
> Pants to view His glorious face.
> Upwards tends to His abode
> To rest in His embrace.

Eileen and I walked back to my family plot and we stood there a while in silence. Will my ashes be spread here one day? Of that, I can't be sure. But the tales were told here, the songs were sung, and as long as my memory has life, I will hold on to that hope.

END

Fa So La Mi

THE FOLLOWING TUNE-
BOOKS ARE REFERENCED BY
NAME OR TUNE:

Christian Harmony, The (1873)
Columbian Harp, The (1812)
Harp of Ages, The (1925)
Hesperian Harp, The (1848)
Millennial Harp, The (1842)
Original Sacred Harp (James 1911)
Sacred Harp, The (1844)
Sacred Harp, The (Cooper 2000)
Sacred Harp, The (Denson 1991)
Shenandoah Harmony, The (2013)
Southern Harmony, The (1854)
Wyeth's Repository (1810)

THE FOLLOWING TUNES ARE
MENTIONED IN THE TEXT,
THE PAGES INDEXED:

Christian Harmony, The (1873)
    408t Shirland 117

Original Sacred Harp (Denson 1966)
    34b The Teacher's Farewell 164
    41 The Spiritual Sailor 164
    84 Masonic Ode 164
    350 The Red Sea Anthem 164

Sacred Harp, The (Cooper 2000)
    38t Sessions 145
    488 Nearer, My God, To Thee
        89, 191
    505 Cleansing Fountain 68, 145,
        178

Sacred Harp, The (Denson 1991)
    28b Wells 213
    29b Tribulation 26, 27, 28, 183
    30b Prospect 66
    34b St. Thomas 145
    37b Liverpool 67
    38b Windham 92
    39t Detroit 216, 217, 220
    40 Lenox 145
    44 The Converted Thief 114
    45t New Britain 85
    47b Idumea 168
    47t Primrose 214
    48b Kedron 114
    49b Mear 145
    50t Mortality 38, 39
    59 Holy Manna 85, 182, 223
    62 Parting Hand 190
    63 Coronation 145
    68b Ortonville 145
    70b Save, Mighty Lord 11, 219
    73t Cusseta 77, 78, 222
    78 Stafford 66, 205
    83b The Dying Minister 115
    84 Amsterdam 63, 64, 145, 224
    89 The Church's Desolation 66
    99 Gospel Trumpet 20
    106 Ecstacy 160
    108b The Traveler 10
    117 Babylon Is Fallen 52
    120 Chambers 116
    121 Florence 45
    122 All Is Well 85
    123t The Dying Christian 115
    131t Messiah 81, 82
    145b Sweet Affliction 51, 148
    147b Laban 145
    155 Northfield 90, 187, 192, 193
    157 Essay 83
    159 Wondrous Love 85, 187, 200
    160t War Department 205
    161 Sweet Home 110
    162 Plenary 9, 151, 152
    178 Africa 187
    179 The Christian Warfare 114
    181 Exit 39

184 Enfield 129
225b Christmas Anthem 129
231 Thou Art Passing Away 115
235 Long Sought Home 72, 223
245 Claremont 187
260 Farewell Anthem 85, 86, 87, 222
268 David's Lamentation 105, 148
269 Bear Creek 197, 198
275b Roll On 66
282 I'm Going Home 168
287 Cambridge 178
288 White 222
312t Sing To Me Of Heaven 170
315 Immensity 148
317 Jackson 66
334 O Come Away 110, 111, 112
376 Help Me To Sing 187
383 Eternal Day 22
384 Panting for Heaven 159
397 Boylstown 145
397 The Fountain 9, 10
398 The Dying Boy 115
399t The Dying Friend 115
410t The Dying Californian 115
417 Weeping Pilgrim 80, 81
428 World Unknown 148
453 Holly Springs 75
454 The Better Land 83, 223
501 O'Leary 196
515 Federal Street 145
522 Ye Heedless Ones 113
523 Pleyel's Hymn (Second) 145
527 My Life And Breath 148
547 Granville 66, 202
551 Jacob's Vision 168, 169

Shenandoah Harmony, The
4b Gravity 206
38 Rome 206
60b In Evil Long 206
66 Night of the Grave 206
76t Doomsday 214
79 Heck 206
101 Madness 206
130 Absent Love 117
140b Ten Thousand Charms 163, 164, 165
140t Jehalah 116
151 Thorn 206
154 Venus 206
165 A Doleful Sound 206
167 Bondage 206
180 Glory Shone Around 206
194 Despair 206
202 Morpheus 206
211 Despair 206
226 Thorny Desert 206
240 Sons of War 206
260t Conflict 153
330t Day of Judgment 206
402 Buzzard's Glory 206
418b Leicester 116

Because tunebooks often change from one printing to the next, we have generally cited the year of the printing of the book confirmed to have contained the tune, or the revision date used by the author in his singing. Where that is not available, the year of first printing is used.

For readers wanting to learn more about or participate in Sacred Harp singing and tradition, these websites will be useful:

FaSoLa.org
OriginalSacredHarp.com
ShenandoahHarmony.com
ShapeNoteSingings.com

By the same author:

Fiction

Big Gurl (Penguin Onyx 1989)

Shock Totem (Penguin Onyx 1990)

Drowning in Fire (Penguin Signet 1992)

This is Your Final Warning (Autonomedia 1992)

Stonecutter (Houghton Mifflin Harcourt 2002)

Wild Ride to Heaven (Houghton Mifflin Harcourt 2003)

Ten Thousand Charms (Houghton Mifflin Harcourt 2005)

Beautiful City of the Dead (Houghton Mifflin Harcourt 2006)

Hydrogen, Sleep and Speed (The Poet's Press 2011)

Meet Me in the Strange (Meerkat Press 2018)

Flaherty's Wake: Abortionist, Boxer, Lawyer, and Priest (Ziggurat 2023)

Non-Fiction

Blood and Volts: Edison, Tesla and the Electric Chair
(Autonomedia 1996, Underworld Amusements 2024)

The Birth of Heroin and the Demonization of the Dope Fiend
(Loompanics Unlimited 1998)

Select Strange and Sacred Sites (Exit 18 Books 2002)

Undercover Mormon: a Spy in the House of the Gods
(Roadswell Editions 2012 [ebook], Ziggurat 2017 [paperback])

Big Noise on the Astral Plane (Ziggurat 2021)

Hakim Bey: Real and Unreal (mogtus-sanlux 2023)

strongsongsofthedead.com

also from the same author...

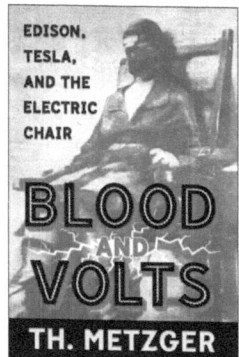

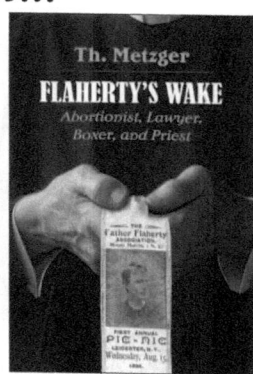

BLOOD AND VOLTS: Edison, Tesla, and the Electric Chair $16
HAKIM BEY: Real and Unreal (mogtus-sanlux) $18
FLAHERTY'S WAKE: Abortionist, Lawyer, Boxer, and Priest (Ziggurat) . . . $16

also from the same publisher...

THE RADICAL BOOK SHOP OF CHICAGO—Kevin I. Slaughter $16
THIS UGLY CIVILIZATION—Ralph Borsodi $20
NEW YORK IS HELL—Benjamin DeCasseres $18

UNDERWORLD AMUSEMENTS

444 MARYLAND AVE. #7940   ESSEX, MD 21221

For postage add $4 for the first item, $1 for each additional.

Or visit WWW.UNDERWORLDAMUSEMENTS.COM

www.ingramcontent.com/pod-product-compliance
Lightning Source LLC
Chambersburg PA
CBHW020444090526
44586CB00045B/847